THE QUEST

IN PURSUIT OF THE ULTIMATE MYSTERY

BY TOM DONGO

Other Books by Tom Dongo

The Alien Tide

*Everything You Wanted to Know
About Sedona in a Nutshell*

Merging Dimensions

The Mysteries of Sedona

Mysterious Sedona

The New Age Frontier

THE QUEST
IN PURSUIT OF THE ULTIMATE MYSTERY

BY TOM DONGO

Light Technology PUBLISHING

Light Technology PUBLISHING

Light Technology Publishing, LLC
Phone: 1-800-450-0985
1-928-526-1345
Fax: 928-714-1132
Mail: PO Box 3540
Flagstaff, AZ 86003
Ship: 4030 East Huntington Drive
Flagstaff, AZ 86004
LightTechnology.com

Dedication

Jacky Stump

Jacky was one of many who have been attracted and held by the mysterious force which is Sedona. He had come from France and was going to experience the vortexes for only a week or so then go on to his next destination. Jacky made many friends while he was in Sedona. He would say his goodbyes and be on his way. Then, just days later, he would re-appear, in Sedona. Every time he tried to leave, he would be drawn back — or had to come back. His Volkswagen van would break down or some other thing would happen so that he had to return.

The universe works in mysterious ways. He ended up being here for over two months. He spent almost his entire summer holiday here. He became a part of Sedona, and Sedona a part of him. That sort of thing happens here. I am certain that there is a high spiritual reason why he found himself here, spent time here and was so affected by Sedona.

Jacky was killed six months later, after returning to France. A native of Switzerland, he worked as a ski mountaineering guide in Val d'Isère, France. He was caught in an avalanche on February 19, 1991, (which ironically is my birthday), in Val d'Isère and died with another skier in his party. He was about 36. Jacky was a rather enigmatic, soft-spoken fellow, charged with an air of mystery derived, no doubt, from his spiritual explorations of sacred sites in Peru, Nepal, Tibet, India and other places. He will forever be missed by all of us who knew him.

A footnote: The motor on Jacky's van went out a few miles from Phoenix Sky Harbor International Airport. Then his flight to France had to return to the airport *three* times as a result of bizarre mechanical problems on two different aircraft. It seems that someone was giving Jacky his last chance to come back to Sedona.

CONTENTS

"Come to the edge," he said.
They said, "We are afraid."
"Come to the edge," he said.
They came.
He pushed them
...and they flew.

— **Guillaume Appolinaire**

2024 Preface

My first book was *Mysteries of Sedona* printed in 1988, and it is still in print thirty-eight years later. Most published books are out of print in five years or less. My only book now out of print (permanently) is *Unseen Beings, Unseen Worlds*. My remaining books in print are *The Alien Tide, The Quest, Mysterious Sedona, The Mysteries of Sedona, Everything You Wanted to Know About Sedona in a Nutshell*, and the very popular *Merging Dimensions*. *Merging Dimensions* describes the super paranormal activity still occurring at the world-famous Bradshaw Ranch near Sedona, Arizona.

At this time, I'm writing the preface for the reprinting of my three books *The Alien Tide, The Quest,* and *Mysterious Sedona*. Much of the content of these books is even more relevant now than when they were originally written. However, since then, a great many changes have taken place in my life as well as local and world events.

I am now one of the world's top UFO and extraterrestrial experts. I have given presentations and spoken at several of the world's biggest UFO/paranormal events such as the international UFO Congress in Las Vegas and the Phenomecon in Vernal, Utah.

At the UFO Congress, I spoke to 600 of the most prestigious UFO researchers in the world about my research, findings, and sightings. I have been a guest on 91 worldwide radio shows — AM, FM, and podcasts. I have been on the famed *Coast to Coast AM* radio program three times recently, which has 30 million primetime listeners.

The events I wrote about in *Mysterious Sedona* are even more acute now than when they were written due to similar events that have occurred around the world since. The world is, as always, a very, very strange place paranormal-wise.

I realized about thirty years ago that I have a very powerful remote-viewing ability. I believe that I was a seer in Tibet lifetimes ago. Remote viewing is simply projecting your subconscious to a place. Time and distance has no relevance when remote viewing. So I see things differently than most people do. The reason I bring up RV is that when I wrote my books, I had been unknowingly using remote viewing.

For several years, the famous author Maureen St. Germain and I taught remote viewing, and we were often very successful. Several of our pupils got to be even better at RV than we were.

I also possess a high psychic ability that I perfected at the Berkeley Psychic Institute in Santa Cruz, California. For two weeks in 2012, I worked on the famous Jacob Wetterling kidnapping case in Minnesota. An informer ended the case, but the FBI said I got further toward solving the case than the world's best psychics.

My personal favorite book is *The Quest*. It's my favorite because of the many testimonials of so many people who were irresistibly drawn to Sedona. And why? The magic is forever there. Enjoy!

PART 1

INTRODUCTION

Mysterious Sedona

by Tom Dongo

I have now spent over five years studying, exploring, cataloging and categorizing unusual occurrences that happen in and around Sedona, Arizona. My two previous books (and various writings) about Sedona are now distributed and sold worldwide. As a result, many thousands of readers have pondered the metaphysical mysteries of Sedona as much as I have. Sedona is, without doubt, an extraordinarily mysterious and mystical place.

This book is a sequel to the first two. It contributes an added dimension to my earlier information. Sedona seems to reflect the best qualities, or perhaps I should say combined qualities, the essences and elements, of the Great Pyramids, Glastonbury, Stonehenge, Ayers Rock, Mt. Shasta, the South American Pyramids, Peru, Tibet, Nepal, India, Lourdes and many other power places around the world. How can I make such a claim? For the reason that I interact on a regular basis with individuals from virtually every corner of the Earth who have spent time in those sacred and mysterious places. Through these travelers I have learned that there is simply no other place like Sedona.

People often undergo major life changes when they come here. Some of these people upon arrival are in emotional distress. And after a few days in Sedona, the causative problem may still exist, whatever and wherever it is, but they are now able to step back, pause, and take a clearer look at what the difficulty actually is. I have observed many individuals make major life decisions and solve major life crises while in Sedona. The decision is usually the right one — they are happy with it. For several years I held various metaphysical-oriented classes and conducted vortex tours in Sedona. For some of the people who came here and joined in my groups, it was their last shot at life. They were ready to give up. There is that mysterious unknown element here in Sedona which changes people — usually in a positive manner. I watched some of these distressed people and I knew what was in store for them (and me). I knew what they were going to go through. There is a saying here that Sedona makes you face everything: either you do and you are victorious and triumphant — or you run. It's not easy. I have seen a lot of it.

There is a very old, widely held statement that our sole purpose for coming into a physical state of existence is to master our emotions. Until that is done, so goes the theory, we cannot progress to higher realms. If so, then Sedona may be playing an even larger role in human evolution than any of us suspect.

Nobody knows precisely what that something is here that makes people change and face their difficulties the way they do. But "it" is real. There are a number of theories of what "it" is. Some are scientific and some are not. Further on in this book you will read the testimonials of twenty-six Sedona residents and learn from them what they have experienced while living here. Testimony is perhaps the most durable proof of all. You can't experience something unless it is in one way or another tangibly real, especially when it involves thousands of people.

Pete Sanders Jr. is a Sedona resident who is also an MIT-trained scientist. He has chosen "to pursue independent research into the limitlessness of the human mental, physical and spiritual potential." Pete asserts that the energy areas of Sedona can best be classified by the terms "inflow" and "upflow." He conducts seminars around the country with a human potential enhancement technique called Free Soul. This technique in part utilizes upflow and inflow energies. According to Pete, upflow energy is primarily found on mesa tops, mountain tops and any area which is significantly higher than the surrounding terrain. Inflow is found in low-lying areas such as valleys, canyons and low-lying caves. He maintains that inflow areas are best for introspection and to cleanse oneself of fears and anxieties, etc. Upflow areas are best for spiritual meditation or direction, due to their uplifting nature. He has been successful with this approach, and it closely agrees with my own thoughts on Sedona's energy areas.

It is also said that Sedona is one of the most magnetically balanced spots on Earth. As I understand it, the benefit of this is that balanced magnetism has a dramatic healing effect, whatever its true source, on a human body. The body allows itself to tune to this magnetic frequency, which seems to be a natural healing frequency. However, I think that this healing effect directs itself more to mental/emotional healings than to physical healings, although I personally know of at least one physical healing which can be attributed only to the Sedona Effect. I will go into that later. I have, though, been witness to many emotional healings here that were, in my opinion, quite miraculous. I have met people burdened with complex emotional difficulties who have had those difficulties literally vanish overnight, even, in some cases, after years of ongoing and expensive professional help which was at best marginally effective. The only explanation for a number of these healings would be the exposure to whatever it is that exists here.

The following example is a physical healing which, in my opinion, can be directly attributed to the mysterious force which exists in Sedona. Four years ago, during the summer, I was employed by two women from out of state to guide them to all the vortex sites. (Vortexes, or vortices, is a generally accepted, rather general term for the Sedona energy phenomena. These vortex energies are localized in certain areas). It was an extensive two-day tour with a lot of hiking involved — about six miles, all told, in widely varying terrain. One of the women, a resilient pioneer type, was in her seventies (I'll call her Marge), she said she could handle the walking all right. But I noticed right away that Marge was periodically very short of breath. She needed to stop and rest quite often. Not a good sign. The second day was as hot as the first; the daytime temperature here is always around 100 degrees in July and August. Toward the end of the second day Marge did not look or act well. At one point she had to lie down for over an hour in the shade of a large piñion pine. By now I knew something was very wrong. It was then that the younger woman admitted to me that Marge had an extremely bad heart and could die any time — at any moment. Marge had been told by her doctors that she had no time left. But Marge had been determined to go to the Sedona red rocks and experience the vortexes even if it meant she was to die here. My first thought was one of irritation and anger at not being told beforehand about her condition, but there wasn't much I could do about it at that point. After an hour or so of rest Marge remarked that she felt much better. She did, in fact, look decidedly improved so we continued on the last mile to the waiting car. As we walked, Marge confessed that she had for some time had an overwhelming, driving desire to come to Sedona and be in the energy here. She added that she really didn't know exactly why. It was just something she had to do.

After the tour Marge and her younger friend went home. One day six months later, by chance, I ran into Marge's friend in Sedona; she had packed up and moved here. I inquired about Marge and her precarious heart condition. She laughed at the question and explained that after visiting Sedona, Marge had returned home and improved so much she got on a plane and went to Europe. She had hiked all over Europe like a teenager. And as far as I know Marge is still going strong. She is one of those people who is a young person locked in an old body. Some people never "get old," and she is one of them.

In addition to many healings of different kinds, past-life remembrances are quite common in the Sedona energy. But in addition to that and perhaps most notable of all is the heightening effect that the Sedona energy has on natural, inherent psychic abilities. It activates, accelerates and enhances psi abilities, often startlingly. Everyone has varying psychic attributes and abilities, and the Sedona Effect can propel those often dormant qualities into full or partial activation. I will ask your patience here and cite some of my own personal experiences as a case in point. The development of my psychic abilities has been fairly remarkable. Before coming to Sedona, my psychic and clairvoyant abilities were average — at best. I did not and do not do "readings." However, I have found myself at times in situations that suddenly demanded all the psychic clarity I could muster to help others or to resolve immediate problems. Early on, when this new psi ability began to unfold, I discovered one day that I could see into the human body like an x-ray machine. People love to test me on this with their maladies, and I am rarely wrong. But this ability, like some others, is one that I have to consciously "turn on." It is not active at all times. Again, I am sure that my own particular psychic expansion has had a great deal to do, or everything to do, with my living in Sedona and being immersed in the mysterious Sedona Effect which inspires, heals and realigns so many. At the same time though, I have also worked hard to accelerate my developing psychic process.

These few following examples of my psychic "hits" are documented and/or were witnessed by others. Several years ago, a California physician and his wife came to Sedona to meet with me. During the conversation he said he had a severe back problem and asked if I would "look" at it. I looked clairvoyantly into the area of his lower spine, and interpreted his (known to him) condition so accurately that he offered, at his cost, to set me up with an office in San Francisco so that I could scan his patients before they went in to see him. I was quite flattered but I declined the offer. I will, rather reluctantly, do future viewing for some people if no harm comes to anyone as a result. I now occasionally delve psychically into areas that I once would not. But I will not intentionally do anything in a psychic sense that will give one person an advantage over another in any way.

In 1991, I predicted the June 28, 1992 California earthquake which was the biggest in California in 40 years. It was 7.4 on the Richter Scale. I had said that there would be a massive earthquake in southern California between June 22 and July 1, 1992. I rarely make predictions.

In 1990, I was shown a missing-person poster of a 28-year-old man who had spent time in Sedona. I had also handled a recent photograph at the same time. Several of his friends were concerned about his welfare and whereabouts. I handed the poster and photograph back. I said that he was dead and his body was lying in a dry wash five miles to the northwest of where they had found his car. At the same time I was shown the photo and poster, I was told that his car had been found in the Mojave Desert in California. My mental vision of the scene looked to me more like northern Arizona or New Mexico. Several weeks ago, in June, 1992, his remains were discovered five miles to the north of where his car had been found — in New Mexico. His remains were lying at the bottom of a dry wash.

Over the phone I predicted a $330,000 land sale for a friend. The property had been on the market a long time. I got the date, the buyer, the places, the amount and the conditions of the sale 100 percent correct. But the down side was that a year later the buyer could not make the payments and the purchase ended up being a financial disaster for all parties. This is one of the reasons I do not like to predict future events — the changeability. You can make a correct prediction one day, and the next day the entire situation can, and often does, reverse itself.

In January of 1992, I discovered that I had developed a remote-viewing ability. I can be in one place, physically, and mentally "see" another physical location hundreds or thousands of miles away. In my mind it appears as a vivid dream, complete with colors, but a part of me is actually there in that location, looking around. I was in Spain in March, '92. A friend who I was with was wondering if everything at his house back in Durango, Colorado was okay. In my mind I went to his house, 6000 miles away and checked the house over completely. I went through each room and all around the outside. I turned to him and said, "The house is fine, but your dog has gotten some paper from somewhere and chewed it up all over the living room floor." The next day he called the person who was checking the house daily. The report was that his dog had pulled books out of the bookcase and chewed them up all over the living room floor.

Shortly before this book went to press, the woman who originally edited this manuscript, Margaret Pinyan, went to Homestead, Florida, to visit her mother who was at the time in poor health. Margaret arrived several days before the disastrous August 24, 1992, hurricane whose wind gusts were clocked at over 200 mph. The hurricane, Andrew, devastated Homestead and Margaret could not be reached, as all phone and power lines were out in southern Florida. After four days, Margaret's friends here in Sedona were becoming justifiably concerned about her health and welfare. I was asked by several of her friends if I would "check on" Margaret to "see" if she was all right. I concentrated for a few seconds and began to see a picture of a house standing relatively intact amidst a surrounding landscape which looked as though it have been subjected to a wartime saturation bombing raid. There was little that was still standing in the entire area — neither trees nor houses. I looked around the area (in my mind) and could see that Margaret was unhurt but was trapped in the area. Two days later Margaret called Sedona to let everyone know that she was fine. Her mother's house was standing and in fair condition, but everything around it had been destroyed by the storm.

Several months ago in a rather urgent situation I located a person and read that person's mind from a distance of 1500 miles in order to obtain needed business information. I was nearly 100 percent accurate. This involved two partners in a business deal and the second partner's whereabouts were not known that evening. The second partner had left a phone message with insufficient information.

All of this psychic enhancement has happened in the time that I have lived in Sedona.

Sedona is world-renowned for its spectacular, towering red rock formations. There are at present around 400 professional artists, writers, sculptors, musicians and photographers living here. Creativity is obviously and definitely enhanced in Sedona, as evidenced by the presence of 400 artists in a city of 12,000 people.

The red rocks are red because they are made up largely of iron oxide — rust. The iron in the rocks is much of the reason for the magnetic quality found here. The iron oxide (or other iron-rich deposits in deeper levels) must be playing a major role in Sedona's paranormal mysteries. What happens here of an extraordinary nature is without doubt confined to the predominately red rock areas. This also applies to UFO activity. For some yet unknown reason, UFOs and ETs are drawn to the red rocks. More on that later. The Sedona enigma will grow and grow. It's been said all along that Sedona would be a spiritual and metaphysical world center, and it is becoming just that.

Dramatic and unusual paranormal incidents happen here in Sedona also. Take, for example, the experience of Sharon Forrest. Sharon Forrest is a well known healer from Montreal who was here conducting a week-long workshop on healing techniques. One day Sharon and most of her group of forty-six had gone on an outing to the vortex at the mouth of Boynton Canyon. Near there, on a ridge, is an 80 foot-tall spire of rock, flat on top, which has been named Kachina Woman. Sharon and a woman friend were standing at the base of Kachina Woman Rock. They were discussing how great it would be to be up there on the top of the rock — the view must be real nice up there. No sooner had they said that, than they were astounded to find themselves, in a blink, standing on the very top of Kachina Woman Rock. They had dematerialized and then rematerialized on the summit of the towering rock spire. Neither one of them knew how it happened, but Sharon is one of those people who has extraordinary things going on around her on a regular basis. They knew they weren't hallucinating because people were running around down below on the flats pointing skyward and shouting exclamations about the two women standing on the top of the lofty spire. A feat which would be difficult even for a well-seasoned rock climber with ropes.

They enjoyed the view for a few minutes and then started to seriously discuss how they were going to get down. They had just finished pondering that when, in a blink, they next found themselves standing on a hillside below the spire, nearly halfway to the parking lot. They had materialized near a man who was in a their group. He came rushing up to them and asked breathlessly how it was they had accomplished such an incredible feat!? The man turned to point to the top of the high rock to say something else and as he did, the two women disappeared and rematerialized again, this time they ended up in the parking lot. The man was absolutely stunned when he turned back and the women had disappeared — again! Many people in the parking lot clustered around the two women and clamored excitedly with all sorts of questions. A lot of people were witness to this event. Sharon still doesn't know exactly how it all happened, although she thinks they had a little help.

The recent (and ancient) Native Americans were aware of the mystical element that exists sin and around what is now Sedona. That is evidenced by what is contained in local Apache and Yavapai folklore and by where they did, and did not, construct their dwellings. The Indians seemed to know where the power spots were and, no doubt, utilized them.

It is a reasonable assumption that the mysterious element, or power, which exists here is a combination of three factors. One: the mysterious and powerful natural energy that exists here; Two: the awesome, inspiring natural scenery that exists here; and Three: the designation by many seeking individuals that Sedona is a spiritual, healing place. That last designation combined with the first two elements make Sedona in reality an inspiring, spiritually unique, healing place. All the ingredients are here. At any rate, whatever may turn out to be the actual source, or cause, the Sedona Effect is genuine. It can, and does, spontaneously affect and change people to the degree that they want to be changed. It's a catalyst fully primed waiting for a medium through which to manifest itself. (But I must include a caution: not every one who comes here has a positive experience. It can also be negative. I think it depends on the desires and attitudes of the one involved).

Sedona is a place where those who are tired of the old come to discover the new.

Sedona, like any mystical destination, also attracts those I will call the Givers. They ask for nothing, and they are seeking nothing. They just seem to know. This is a mysterious nomadic breed of people who, after they have gone, leave you wondering deeply who they really were. One such person was a man who came to Sedona owning only the clothes he wore on his body and what he carried in a small cloth sack. He was mute. He could not speak, although I suspect that his silence was by choice and not because of a physical deficiency. He was a healthy, handsome, fit-looking fellow in his mid-thirties with long brown hair and a trim, well-kept beard. He called himself Light. I have no idea what his given name was. He would communicate by hand gestures and quickly scribbled notes on tiny pads of paper he always carried with him. He preferred not to live in man-made buildings, but instead lived in caves wherever he went, if possible. He preferred caves, he said. He liked to be close to the Earth, in any kind of weather. Whoever met the man loved him — everyone did. He was not the usual person who was aggressively pursuing the Great American Dream of the biggest, best and most expensive of everything. He owned only what he could carry ... and he envied no one. He had a peace, a charismatic Christlike serenity about him that I think would be the envy of just about every harried, stressed-out executive who drives 60 miles on a congested freeway every day to make his or her $60,000 a year. Then one day Light said he had somewhere else to go. I think it was somewhere in Tennessee. And he was gone. We wondered for weeks who he really was — and we missed his energy. I have run across a few people, men and women, like Light. He was, and is, not a common man.

I mentioned earlier that UFOs are also drawn to the Sedona area. UFO activity here isn't confined exclusively to the red rock areas, but if you drew a circle around the red rocks (about ten miles across) where most of the activity is, and then drew a second circle ten miles farther out, you would be encompassing probably 80 percent to 90 percent of all the UFO sightings that occur, or are reported, in northern Arizona. In the past six months, from February, 1992, to the end of July, 1992 (when this was written), there have been almost constant UFO sightings here, probably more sightings than in the past five years combined. Almost weekly there are major sightings in the local area. These UFO "flaps" tend to flare up and continue for a period of time, then taper off or abruptly cease altogether. I suspect that is what will happen with this current flap, although at the moment it shows no sign of abating.

I write a monthly column entitled "UFOs, ETs and You" in the *Sedona Journal of Emergence*. The Sedona Journal is distributed internationally, so my stories have a wide readership. Two years after I arrived in Sedona, my focus of purely metaphysical/spiritual pursuits was combined with an additional focus on researching UFO and alien activity. I could barely avoid it. I was surrounded by UFO/paranormal occurrences, so I had, and have, a fertile resource to draw from. Plus, I have acquired an overpowering and, unrelenting curiosity. It is a most incredible opportunity to be able to chase such elusive enigmas as UFOs and aliens and attempt to arrive at some sort of rational explanation of what they are, why they are, and how they must involve all of us.

At the end of this book are reprints of portions or entire columns of my *Sedona Journal* articles. Much UFO coverage is included in those reprints. I firmly suspect that the highest levels of divinity or spirituality, are integrally linked with most UFOs and UFO activity. I think we are in store for some major surprises in that area in the future.

I hope you enjoy the following pages and perhaps gain new or reinforcing insights about Sedona from these delightful local residents who have graciously chronicled their personal experiences in this book.

One of the most frequently discussed topics in Sedona is why it is that so many spiritually based people are irresistibly drawn here. People often give up everything in order to come here. Perhaps this book will add yet another piece to a very large puzzle — a very mysterious puzzle, at that.

PART 2

UFOS, ETS , AND YOU

Stories from the
Sedona Journal of Emergence,
selected from fifty-one articles
written over a five-year period

SEDONA
Journal of EMERGENCE!
$4.95
$6.50 CANADIAN
MARCH 1996
ETS, UFOS, THE HOTTEST LATEST GALACTIC NEWS PLUS THE SECRET GOVERNMENT, THE
PHOTON BELT & THE GULF BREEZE SIX! · CHANNELING FROM YHWH, KRYON, LAZARIS
AND RAMTHA! ZOOSH PLUS ARCHANGELS, VYWAMUS & ASHTAR COMMAND
FEATURES ON MAYAN CALENDAR, REINCARNATION, HEALING, ASTROLOGY, SWAMI
PREDICTIONS ON
EARTH CHANGES · THE WEATHER · HUMAN ENERGY · AND MORE!

UFO Crash in Sedona?

July 25, 1994

During the Memorial Day weekend of May 28–30, 1994, an event of national significance occurred near Sedona, Arizona. The information I have gathered points to several probabilities. I think what occurred was either the crash of a UFO, a major landing of a UFO, the downing of a jet fighter by a UFO or vice versa, or something else which may have been a combination of any of the above.

A friend in Air Force Intelligence (generally known as O.S.I.) once said to me that in an intelligence investigation if as few as two circumstantial events point directly to a separate probable event, then the separate event is assumed as fact and the investigation proceeds from there. That is the point I have arrived at here. All evidence, both direct and circumstantial, points to the landing, crash or otherwise, of an airborne object of extreme interest to the U.S. military and our national government. Quoting from a letter to a Cottonwood, Arizona, UFO researcher from a Nevada private investigator who had knowledge of the details of an event during its occurrence: "I just happen to think that you might be sitting on top of the hottest opportunity to expose a covert government operation that's ever come along. This has the possibility of becoming the most definitive exposé ever to surface revealing government and ET-related activities. The Roswell incident [the Roswell, New Mexico UFO crash of

1947] could be a second-rate story compared to this." In a few sentences I think that statement accurately sums up the Sedona area Memorial Day weekend series of occurrences.

Related incidents and sightings point to the days between May 25 and June 2 as being the key period. I am going to present in chronological order this information I have gathered and my own conclusions. Because there was nowhere to go externally for answers to the puzzling sightings and experiences being reported, other sources of information were sought. Therefore, following the accounts I have written about these occurrences are channeled viewpoints from trusted sources. I purposely and intentionally did not and do not want to know what the channels reported, as I did not want it to influence my writing and research in any way. So what I have written is totally separate from the channeled material and is presented from a rather clinical research perspective.

The strange events of the 1994 Memorial Day weekend began for me personally in this manner: About 11:00AM on Sunday, May 29, I was driving northeast in the left lane on highway 89A entering Sedona when a tractor-trailer rig passed me in the right lane — the slow lane. The truck was going about ten miles an hour over the posted 40 mph speed limit. The cab itself was ordinary and a drab white color. But the flatbed trailer it was pulling drew my attention. Being a researcher of the unusual and one who is naturally curious anyway, I look at and take note of anything out of the ordinary. When the white cab passed me, I got a good look at the flatbed it was hauling. What was extremely odd about it was the cover material over the load. I had never seen anything like it. It was a thick olive-drab plastic, stretched so tight that it looked like Saran Wrap stretched over a platter of cut-up vegetables. The plastic was the same color and thickness as a Vietnam body bag once so often shown on television. There was one round object standing upright in the center of the load that was about four feet high and appeared to be hollow. It was about 30 inches in diameter and looked quite sharp, similar to a length of steel pipe.

The plastic must have been extremely strong, as it was not torn by the edges of this round object. When truckers cover a flatbed load they usually use inexpensive, clear plastic tarpaulins or plain or waterproof

Courtesy of Miller Johnson

canvas tarps. When the odd flatbed passed me I had not yet heard any current reports of strange sightings in the Sedona area. The highly unusual tarp, however, stuck in my mind. Shortly after I got home came a flood of information from many sources. The town was beginning to buzz with strange stories. Too much was happening too fast to be the work of a few paranoid or intentional rumor-makers.

There was an urgent phone message to call a woman friend who is a UFO investigator in Cottonwood. Cottonwood is a city of about 6,000 people fifteen miles southwest of Sedona. I returned her call that afternoon of the 29th. As soon as she picked up the phone she exclaimed, "Do you know what is happening around here?!" She was so excited that I was instantly alerted and at the same time a little miffed that I didn't know what "it" was. (I am usually the first one around here to hear dramatic news of any kind.) Turns out she had been investigating the stories for two days. She continued with startling news of dozens of military helicopters landing on the ground in Cornville; FBI all over Sedona; dead, possibly mutilated cattle found on House Mountain; UFOs flying over Cottonwood daytime and nighttime; and a group of mountain bikers being stopped and turned back at gunpoint near the mouth of Secret Canyon by the U.S. military with M-16 assault rifles. She went on to say that Senators Dole and Mitchell had been seen in Sedona a week before all this unusual activity began. I was not expecting such an avalanche of stimulating news and was a bit speechless at first. I thanked her for calling me, and we agreed to stay in close contact to share information and see what else might develop in the meantime.

While I stood there trying to integrate this bewildering information and make some sense of it, the phone rang. The call was from a woman in Tucson, also a UFO researcher, who exclaimed in a concerned, agitated tone, "Tom, what the hell is going on in Sedona? I just got a call from a friend in the U.S. Senate. I was told that there was some sort of an incident, maybe involving a UFO, near Sedona and that the military was preparing to seal off all routes into and out of Sedona. What's going on?" My Tucson friend, who knew nothing of the other incidents being reported in the Sedona area, could not have been influenced by those stories. I asked her if her Senate friend knew what had happened here. She replied that her friend might have known, but didn't tell her. I got the impression that her friend wanted to leak information but was afraid to be more specific. It could be, I thought, that her friend in the Senate was, like everyone else, just trying to find out what was going on.

My investigator/researcher brain shifted into high gear as I began to smell a UFO crash. I have been near this sort of thing before. I knew the signs. And I knew I had to move fast before the trail got cold. In the UFO business, hours or days can mean the difference between a major event or a cold, unverifiable rumor. I started calling people on the phone and asking lots of questions. One thing quickly led to another, and I had more and more pieces of the puzzle. At the time I was also all too well aware of the military's quick-recovery teams. These teams are stationed around the country and can be mobilized and at the site of a UFO crash in a matter of hours. When one of these teams arrives at a crash site, they clean up the site so well that it is generally restored to its original condition.

I am asked sometimes how a UFO can possibly crash, given their technology. For one thing, it's evident that they occasionally do have mechanical problems, sometimes with disastrous results, such as the presently well-published UFO crashes at Aztec, New Mexico; Roswell, New Mexico; and Kecksburg, Pennsylvania. I have also seen on videotape a Russian Air Force colonel (in uniform) vehemently telling an American UFO researcher that both the U.S. and the Russians have particle-beam weapons fully capable of shooting down an alien spaceship. The Russian colonel demonstrated, on camera, a small version of their beam weapon. It was impressive. He said the Americans have an operative beam weapon that is far more destructive than the one they have. A close associate and friend of mine who is an American Air Force colonel says he watched as one of these U.S. beam weapons was being readied for firing, although he did not see it in operation.

The question is, are they shooting back? I think so, because the Russian colonel said that in a Soviet effort to collect a UFO, three of their most advanced M.I.G. fighters were shot down by UFOs. He says they now have a hands-off policy toward UFOs.

Speed, prudence and caution are my guidelines, because I know what I might be dealing with. During the course of my investigation a man told me that he had heard that several roads out in the desert had been blocked by military vehicles. I had no way to verify this report/rumor, but what gave it a measure of credibility was that I heard the rumor before anyone else knew what the Tucson woman had told me. I was the first local person to hear of the possibility of Sedona being sealed off.

It seems that a hornet's nest of UFO and paranormal-type activity was stirred up that Memorial Day weekend. I am certain that most, if not all of it, was directly connected even though some of the reports seemed to be unrelated. I say that because all of what I narrate here occurred during a period of about ten days, with Memorial Day the focus. Those events are as follows, as close as I could put them in chronological order.

On May 29 at 8:23PM a red-ringed UFO was seen moving in unusual aerial patterns in the eastern sky as seen from Cottonwood. This UFO was watched by four adults and was described as glowing and pulsating. Then two smaller, white-glowing objects flew directly over the four witnesses at a high rate of speed. One UFO was flying straight, but the other was erratic, as though it were having some sort of control problem. Both

House Mountain from the south.

white UFOs then disappeared into a cloud. The red-ringed object had also moved out of sight. That same evening at 10:22PM — again from Cottonwood — nine adult witnesses observed two red-ringed UFOs flying seemingly in a search pattern for one and one-half hours in the direction of House Mountain. House Mountain lies halfway between Sedona and Cottonwood and is adjacent to the small settlements of Cornville and Page Springs. During the course of my investigation several people had asked, "How come all this stuff didn't appear in the local newspapers?" My answer was that the mainstream media ignore UFO activity and stories these days, and even if somebody dragged a spaceship into town behind their pickup, newspapers probably wouldn't report it.

In a separate sighting that Sunday night, four adults watched two orange balls of light fly at high altitude over Cottonwood and disappear to the southwest over Mingus Mountain. This was at 11:45PM. I might add here that the "UFOs" the U.S. government has been flying at the supersecret Area 51 base 100 miles north of Las Vegas in almost every instance glow a bright orange color. It seems that these UFOs have either been

House Mountain from the west.

constructed with alien help or been "back engineered," meaning built or reconstructed by salvaging a crashed (or donated) alien craft. These craft, it seems, are being flown by U.S. military personnel or are a joint venture by U.S. and alien pilots. I have an excellent nighttime color photo taken by a California physicist of one of these very same Area 51 craft. Were these orange balls of light that were flying over Cottonwood U.S. government craft? I think they were. Either that or the same ships being flown by aliens.

Also on May 29, a Cottonwood man and his wife watched a single glowing orange object slowly fly over Cottonwood at an altitude of approximately 6000 feet. They remarked that the UFO was very bright orange and moved south at a leisurely speed. At 9:30 P.M. on the same night the red-ringed UFOs were again seen, this time near House Mountain, which is 5127 feet high from a base elevation of about 4000 feet. It is an expansive, rather rounded and unpopulated desert mountain with a base circumference of approximately ten miles. That same evening, also at 9:30PM, a dark UFO "the size of a football field" with two blinking lights on either end flew slowly east between House Mountain and Camp Verde. Witnesses said this object flew in a slow, sweeping motion, and while it was in view two red-glowing UFOs were seen hovering far above the enormous dark UFO. This lasted for over 40 minutes before the three objects disappeared in the distance. The next day (May 30) two black military helicopters were seen flying around the same area where the one large and two smaller UFOs had been seen the night before.

During the entire three-day Memorial Day weekend, U.S. Apache and Cobra attack helicopters were flying at low altitude, particularly in the Sedona area. They were flying, patrol fashion, in groups of two to six. At one point five Apache helicopters flew in a line south to north over Sedona at a height of 300 feet or less. These are loud, powerful helicopters. I spoke to an ex-military man who told me that some of the helicopters he saw over Sedona that weekend were combat-ready, with loaded rocket launchers. Four of these helicopters flew over me and were indeed equipped with loaded rocket launchers and, in my opinion, seemed to be looking for something to shoot at.

Again that Sunday holiday, a group of four women UFO researchers who had been noticing the odd activity around House Mountain decided to go there to investigate. They had driven along the road on the south and west sides of the mountain and had seen nothing unusual. Deciding to return to Cottonwood in early afternoon, they were near Cornville when two black cars came racing up behind them at a high rate of speed. Both approaching cars, the women said, were shiny black, new, and each had short antennas sticking out both the driver's and the passenger's side windows. One black car passed the four women and pulled in front — close. The women were now boxed in between the two black cars, both driven by men and displaying black Arizona license plates with white numerals. Black Arizona plates are unusual; they are normally maroon with white numerals. The two black cars followed the women researchers for about five minutes; then the car following them pulled out and passed. Both cars then accelerated down the narrow highway. The women estimated that the two cars were going over 80 mph as they sped out of sight on the narrow, curving rural highway.

The women, again curious and thinking they were in the clear, went back to House Mountain to look around some more. They turned off on unpaved National Forest Road 120, which leads into a remote area where several dead cattle had been found the day before by a local man. He said the cattle may have been mutilated UFO style, but not being an expert in that field, he could not be sure. On one long, open section of 120 were the imprints of a wide-tracked vehicle. The tracks went off into the desert, coming to an end behind an area with thick brush. In itself this was odd because there was no evidence of work being done on the gravel road by maintenance crews. Ranchers do not use tracked vehicles in this area. They almost exclusively use four-wheel-drive or two-wheel-drive pickup trucks.

The four women then made a wide loop around House Mountain, taking photos as they went. They continued on State Highway 179 into the Village of Oak Creek, then on into Sedona, turning left onto State Route 89A to return to Cottonwood. As the women were passing the Sedona city limits, two black military helicopters appeared out of nowhere and began pacing them. The helicopters followed them fifteen miles, all the way to Cottonwood. They even followed them along the winding back roads to the home of one of the women. This activity was witnessed by the husband of one of the women. He remarked that from his higher vantage point it was obvious that these two black multimillion-dollar military helicopters had been following them. The question is, why? Did the four women get too close to something they were not supposed to see? All of the photographs taken by the women that afternoon came out black. Photos on that same roll of 35-mm film taken several days before developed normally. This has happened before around here during UFO activity. It takes strong radiation to black out a roll of film like that. In one other case I know of similar to the four women's experience, it was obvious that some sort of device was "beamed" toward the photographer. The photographer in the second case was shooting photos of a ball of white light hovering near her in the open desert near Sedona.

That same day, again on Sunday, May 29, a Cornville man driving east on rural route 119 between Cornville and McGuireville saw in the distance over a dozen military helicopters on the ground. This report says that the man counted seventeen helicopters sitting on a high mesa between

House Mountain and McGuireville. This would have been about two air miles from where the four women researchers were that day when photographing and tracking imprints of a large, tracked vehicle and subsequently followed by two military helicopters. It seems those seventeen helicopters were positioned in a staging area ready to move at a moment's notice to a nearby area. Near what? Why? Why would seventeen combat-type helicopters be concentrated in one unlikely rural area far from the nearest air base, which would have to be either Luke Air Force Base or the partly decommissioned Williams Air Force Base in Phoenix, 130 miles away? With all the unusual activity around the south side of House Mountain that weekend, it would be a safe assumption that that was one of the areas, or the single area, upon which the military was focusing its attention.

To backtrack a bit, about ten days before Memorial Day weekend, radio station KFYI in Phoenix reported that Senators Dole and Mitchell were seen in Sedona and were allegedly engaged in a high-level, supersecret meeting of some sort. This clandestine meeting ties in nicely with the unusual events the weekend of May 29–30. Coincidentally with this, a retired man in Colorado who spends a great deal of his time following clandestine government activity called an associate of mine and said that he had just heard a rumor that the U.S. government was preparing to move some of its functions and operations to the Sedona area. Again, so many diverse and extraordinary occurrences happened in such a short time span that one has to assume a connection.

Furthermore, on Memorial Day weekend one of the largest hotels in Sedona was booked solid by FBI agents on short notice — so many agents that a person had to be assigned to locate lodgings for them in other area motels and hotels. What were Senators Dole and Mitchell, a raft of FBI agents and 17 attack helicopters doing in the Sedona area, in an out-of-the-way, rather average American town in the same time frame? Those activities alone suggest something of extreme significance, something the general public was not informed of, to be sure.

This next incident took place in Sycamore Canyon, a 33-mile-long canyon three miles northeast of Cottonwood. This incident happened on Memorial Day, the 30th. I'll call this man Ray. Ray is in his late twenties and is the son of a local rancher. Deciding to hike into Sycamore Canyon, he left the ranch at 7:30 in the morning. The going was a little slower than he had anticipated, so that he was only about halfway to his destination by late afternoon. The sun was low on the horizon when he noticed that high up in the cliffs something was following him. He said that whatever it was, it glowed white and was somewhat bell-shaped. It seemed to be trying not to be seen. Then things really got strange. He said that he soon came upon the carcass of a dead animal about the size of a young coyote. The carcass probably weighed about twenty pounds. What was odd about it, he said, was that it had not been dead long and looked like an animal that was half cat and half fox or coyote. Even more odd was the fact that its stomach seemed to have been removed by someone or something — there was only loose skin and a hollow cavity where the stomach had been.

As he continued down the canyon, high above and to the right two white-glowing, triangular-shaped craft appeared. They made no sound and seemed to float along the canyon rim high above him. Then, he said, it took him five or six hours to walk a distance of just over a mile. He doesn't remember, but he feels he may have had as much as five hours of missing time.

This is not the first time this sort of thing has happened there. Almost an identical incident involving two Cottonwood men took place ten years ago in the same general area. Ray did not know these men.

A week before May 30 a local couple had gone to an isolated location to inspect some property they were interested in purchasing. There were a number of buildings on the sale property, and as they were going through the buildings they discovered some papers on the floor of one of them, a small cottage. Most of the papers had handwriting on them and appeared to have been left by someone who had spent some time in the cottage. On one of the sheets of paper was written "Abduction is the Art of the Kidnapper." A connection to Ray's experience?

Two other Memorial Day weekend reports involved people being stopped at gunpoint by military personnel deep in the canyons west of Sedona. Before I go into those incidents I should explain the topography of the Sedona area to give the reader a better mental reference. To the south of Sedona is mostly open desert, with a few high, forested mountain ranges spaced here and there all the way to Mexico. To the north and east lies the Mogollon Rim, which is the southernmost edge of the Colorado Plateau — the largest plateau in the world. The Mogollon Rim is an almost vertical wall, created by earth movement in prehistory, and is punctuated here and there by a series of canyons. The Rim is at an elevation of 6000 feet, whereas Sedona's elevation is 4500 feet. To the west of Sedona are the famous canyonlands. These are Sterling Canyon, Bear Sign Canyon, Secret Canyon, Long Canyon, HS Canyon, Boynton Canyon, Fay Canyon, Red Canyon, Hartwell Canyon and Lincoln Canyon. Most of these canyons originate at Secret Mountain, which can be likened to the hub of a wagon wheel. The deeper canyons are like spokes radiating to the east, west and south. The Colorado Plateau connects to Secret Mountain from the north.

In one incident three people were riding mountain bikes on May 28 and suddenly encountered a number of military types dressed in black uniforms with no insignia, armed with M-16 military assault rifles. The bikers were about a mile from the mouth of Secret Canyon. They were told they were in an area they shouldn't be (this is in Coconino National Forest) and to turn around and go back the way they had come. They did. I have since learned that the U.S. military, at least elite units, do indeed wear black uniforms when guarding sensitive areas or installations. I have been told by an ex-army intelligence officer that elite army units do operate in the Secret Canyon area. Furthermore, I have been told by another military source that military personnel have to have a top-secret clearance to go into that area. Why? No one knows.

On the 29th or 30th I got a report that two off-duty policemen were hiking to the east of Secret Canyon in nearby Sterling Canyon and ran into a young, armed, U.S. Marine who reportedly told the two officers they could go no further. This is the tenth incident of this type I know of that has occurred in that same general area in the past five years. I have been told by a military source that a U.S. citizen (or anyone else) has a lawful right to demand, in a situation such as I just mentioned, the soldier's name, rank and specific orders as to why he is there. But, I suppose, with an M-16 pointed at your nose you're not likely to want to push it.

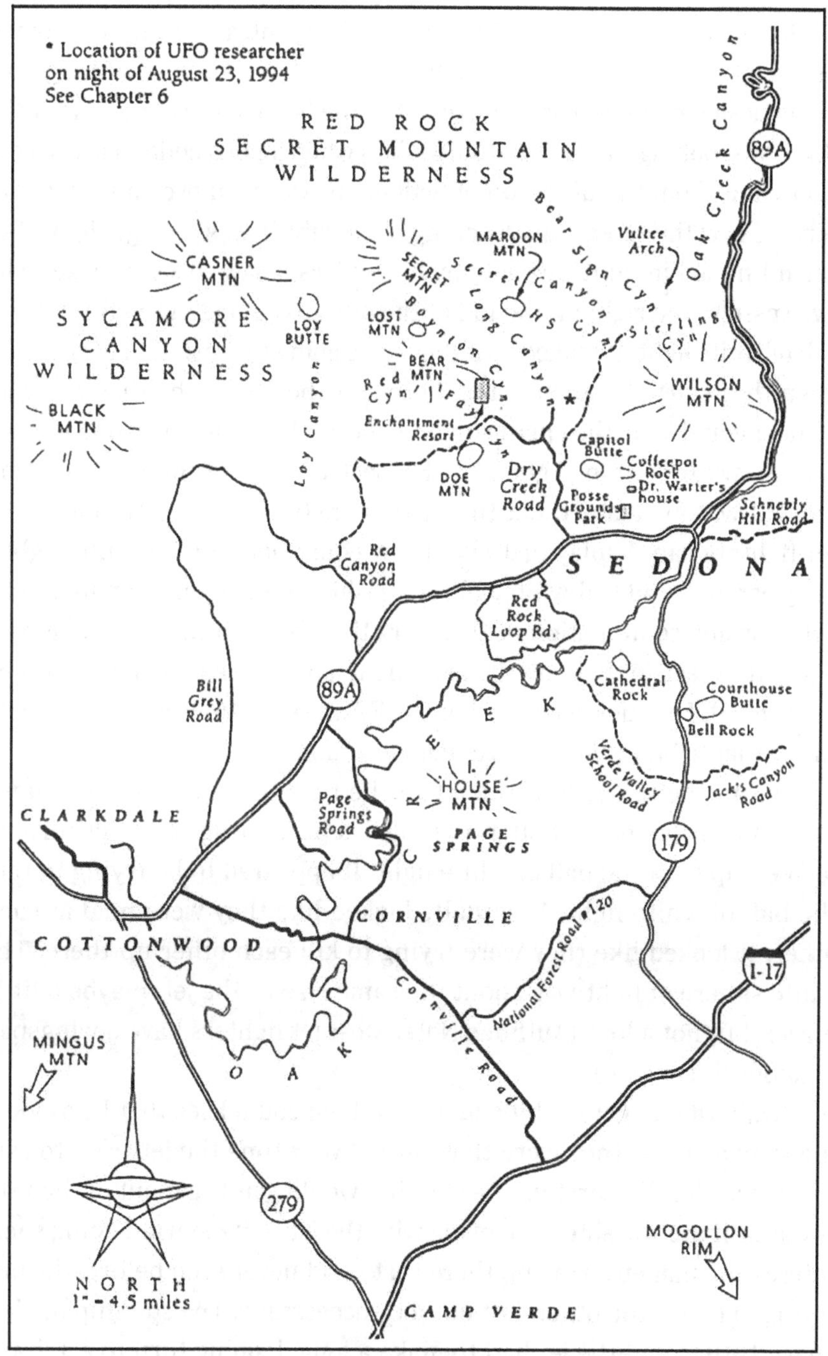

Map of Secret Canyon area.

In yet another Memorial Day weekend incident, a Cottonwood woman gave me the following report in a taped interview. "At 9:35PM May 30 my son (a design engineer) and I were out in the front yard star gazing at the sky. I was looking through my binoculars when all of a sudden a streak of light came from the direction of Sedona. It was soon over my driveway. When I saw the streak approaching, I thought it was a single light. But when I honed in on it through my binoculars, I saw that it was actually two vessels, one right on the tail of the other. The one in the front was a ball of white light. It looked as if they were going to crash into each other. Then they started maneuvering. I thought the one in the rear was a jet plane. I could hear the engine on one but not the other. The one in back had two white running lights. I had expected to see red or green, which I thought was mandatory, but the lights were both white." (Author's note: Jet fighters can display just about any combination of running lights. They can be steady all-white, all-red, flashing red, green or white strobe lights or any combination of these or still other mixed combinations. I have often seen jet fighters flying at night at high speed with no running lights at all. I am not certain what the F.A.A. regulations are, but I would wager that fighter pilots ignore them at will.)

"From the tail end of the jet in the rear there was a continuous red glow or flame, as though the pilot kept igniting the afterburners to keep up with the ball of white light. It appeared to be trying to ram the ball of white light. It actually looked like they were mad at each other. It looked like they were trying to kill each other up there. The white sphere of light was about the same size as the jet, maybe a little bigger, but not a lot." (Author's Note: Most jet fighters have a wingspan of about thirty feet.)

"Only when I got my binoculars on them could I see that I was looking at two crafts, they were that close. Every time the jet tried to ram the, what I'll call, starship, the starship would gently get out of the way. It was as if the starship was toying with the jet. They started doing some interesting maneuvering up there that I had never seen before, the one trying to follow the other, but not too successfully. The starship made a sharp U-turn and the jet had to make a long, looping turn to catch up. The starship headed in the direction of Sedona. The jet caught up with it and they both looked as one light again as they disappeared into the distance."

The next day, Tuesday the 31st, at 4:20AM Cheryl K., a Sedona resident, was on her way to Phoenix. She was halfway to Cottonwood on Highway 89A (near where the UFO and jet fighter were last seen) when she came up behind a trailer rig making a right turn onto Red Canyon Road, also known locally as Two Trees Road. What was unusual about this rig was that the truck was towing a piggy-back trailer — two flatbed trailers instead of one. She evidently knows trucks, because she said that this one had additional struts under each flatbed in order to support an extremely heavy load. (By law, 60,000 pounds is the legal load limit for a trailer rig. This one could have carried twice that weight — 120,000 pounds or more. Evidently this one could do just that, as she remarked that the truck was also unusually large. Military tractor trailers are bigger and they can pull far more weight than a public or commercial rig.) The large rig turned off 89A and headed toward Red Canyon.

Just a few days after that, a man who lives in the Red Canyon area was returning home at 10:30 in the evening. On that narrow and unpaved desert road, he came up behind a piggy-back trailer rig. It looked brand new, he said, and it was pulling two flatbed trailers. On each flatbed was a bright yellow, tall, boxlike container. There was a pickup truck leading the rig, and both big and small trucks pulled over and stopped when the local man drove up behind them. The man said that the whole thing was very strange. It seemed as if the trucks did not want him following them or getting too good a look at what they were hauling or where they were going. As the man slowly drove around them, he said he got a pretty good look at the whole setup. He added that there was absolutely no reason for a rig like that to be out there. There was no construction or anything else anywhere near that area that could explain its presence. I checked with some of the residents who live in that area. They agreed that there was no logical reason why a truck like that would be out there.

The local man passed the truck with the yellow containers and the leading pickup truck. He drove slowly along the road ahead to see where they were going. From a distance he watched the two trucks turn left onto

Red Canyon Road and head toward Highway 89A, the same road Cheryl K. saw the empty trailer rig turn off 89A onto Red Canyon Road. The obvious question is, what was in the two yellow boxes on the flatbed trailers and where did they pick up or drop off their load?

I am going to include at this point some later sightings that I believe are directly related to the Memorial weekend events. On June 12, 1994, in the Page Springs/Cornville area, a dozen or so residents watched for thirty minutes a silver cylindrical UFO moving back and forth over House Mountain as if it were looking for something. Also on June 12, a Cottonwood woman observed a silvery-gold cylindrical UFO fly over Mingus Mountain heading northeast in the direction of House Mountain. On June 2 a helicopter pilot flying over a remote forested region west of Prescott (50 miles southwest of Sedona) said that he flew over a large contingent of military troops in an area where he felt troops should not be.

In the early spring of 1994 on a half-dozen separate occasions, airliner-sized military cargo planes were seen flying at treetop level across the desert near Red Canyon — usually at two or three in the morning. This was in conjunction with dozens of black military helicopters doing the same thing over an eight- or nine-month period. One black military helicopter intimidated a remote homeowner to the point where the man, out of frustration, got his shotgun and was going to try to shoot it down. The last straw was when the helicopter hovered ten feet over his house. The helicopter left when the man pointed his shotgun at the pilot. Also during this eight- or nine-month period there was an eerie buzzing/vibrating sound whose source could not be determined, from below ground or from the air. I've heard this sound myself, and it is indeed strange. This tone, or sound, moves in a linear, east-west direction from Secret Canyon to Lincoln Canyon, a distance of about five miles. It has also been experienced far out into the flat desert near the canyons. It has at times been so intense as to shake buildings for hours at a time, to the point of completely distracting the residents of those areas. There is no natural phenomenon that can readily explain this sound.

A Cornville woman, on a Thursday morning in early July, experienced a dramatic sighting on her way to work at 9:30AM. As she described the event, she was approaching the intersection of 89A and the Page Springs/Cornville road when she saw a low-flying aircraft — which, by her description, was a delta-winged fighter bomber with clusters of rockets under both wings. The jet fighter passed low and to the left of her car and began to make a slow, rolling upward turn. It was tilted at about a twenty-degree angle toward her — one wing up, one down. She said she had an unobstructed view of the plane, and it was a clear, cloudless day. She described to me how the plane banked and started to gain altitude. As the plane moved up, something on the middle right side of the aircraft flashed, as if a large part of the craft was mirrorized and the sun had reflected off it. She said there was this bright flash and then the jet simply disappeared, vanished into thin air. She waited five minutes to see if the plane would come around again or be seen in the distance. She did not see it again. She emphasized to me that most of the top of the delta-winged fighter was in full view, not traveling downward away from her.

The last two items I am sure somehow tie in to everything else in this report. On May 19, a week before Memorial Day weekend, a local, long-time wilderness guide and I were going east in a four-wheel-drive vehicle on the Vultee Arch Road just past the trailhead into Secret Canyon. This was a bright, clear day and the time was 10:30AM An animal walked out in front of the vehicle and stopped to look at us, about 50 feet away. It probably weighed between twenty and twenty-five pounds. The animal looked as if it were half cat and half canine. It had short front legs and longer hind legs, which gave it a cheetah-like appearance, and a long upward-curled, bottle-brushlike tail. The hair on the tail looked about two inches long, wiry and sparse. Its body was grayish brown, and over most of its face was an almost apelike cream-colored patch. The face was foxlike, with a long, thin snout, small nose and foxlike eyes. The ears were like that of a cat, small and pointed. We both got a very good look at this animal, and neither of us had ever seen an animal like it. My friend made the remark that as far as he knew, an animal like that did not exist anywhere on Earth. In appearance and size it was very similar to the one Ray had found dead in Sycamore Canyon 15 miles to the west of our sighting. I checked books on Southwest animals and the only one that came close was a coatimundi. It was not a coatimundi.

Another odd animal sighting took place on July 8 near Red Canyon itself. Two local residents were driving on Red Canyon Road when an animal walked out of desert brush into the headlights of their pickup truck. A very good depiction of this animal was drawn in pencil for me. The animal was taller than a hundred-pound dog that belonged to the driver of the pickup. It had very long, shaggy hair over all of its body and a long, horselike shaggy tail. It had catlike ears and a rounded, wide catlike face. Nothing like either of these two animals normally exists around here.

* * *

These following events, sightings and incidents occurred during the weeks after the main body of this story was written. This update was added on August 8, 1994.

On July 13, a Cornville man who lives a few miles south of House Mountain had this very unusual experience. Late that night, he said, "a golf ball-sized sphere of light came up to my bedroom window and seemed to be looking in at me." He told me that the little ball of light seemed either to have intelligence or was intelligently controlled. He added that the tiny sphere was so bright that it lit up everything in the immediate area. His girlfriend also witnessed this episode, but from a window in a different part of the house. After four or five seconds the ball of light drifted away from the house in a zig-zag manner and then over some horses in a corral. The sun-like little ball lit up the entire backyard as it went over the horses, but the horses paid no attention; either they couldn't see it or they were not afraid of it.

During a public book signing of my four books at the Loft bookstore in Sedona on July 16, a man called from California to tell me about a most amazing sighting he had witnessed in Boynton Canyon recently. (He has a Ph.D. and is in the top management of one of this country's biggest defense contractors specializing in space and guided-missile technology.) He told me that he had seen a UFO slowly disappear into a high canyon wall in Boynton Canyon. As he was describing this incident to me, local resident Mason Rumney came in. He is the only other person I know of who has had a nearly identical experience. Coincidence? I passed the phone to Mason along with a brief explanation. The two men talked for over a half-hour about their similar dramatic sightings.

It seems that during the latter part of July, in the Jerome area (near Cottonwood) there were men and women working in pairs who were asking questions about UFO sightings and whether there were any group meetings in the area to discuss UFO activity. The conversation of these odd couples sounded as though they were reading from a script.

It now turns out that there were two witnesses to the vanishing of a delta-winged, triangular jet fighter-bomber. The second sighting was by a physician's wife near Sedona. It was early July, she said, that the triangular jet fighter vanished into thin air as she watched it. So there were two witnesses in different places and times who do not know each other but who each have experienced the same event.

In two other clearly related incidents, a woman and her two sons watched as two jet fighters and a UFO vanished into thin air. On the night of July 27, this local woman and her two sons were on a remote hill near Red Canyon that overlooks a vast area of desert and canyons. They had gone out to look for UFOs. They said that at 9:40PM a white-glowing UFO appeared and flew slowly in the area of Red Canyon and Secret Mountain. The UFO would disappear for minutes at a time as it went behind towering rock formations and in and out of adjacent canyons. Then about 10PM, a fast jet fighter suddenly appeared from the northeast at the same time as a second fighter appeared from the west. The woman and her sons watched the UFO come out into the open and accelerate rapidly toward the southwest. The two converging jets caught up and stayed with the UFO for three or four seconds. Then the three craft disappeared. The three witnesses added that the roar of the fighters' engines also ceased at that instant, and they fully concur on the accuracy of the sequence of events.

To make matters really interesting, the same night at almost the same time, a former Vietnam helicopter pilot watched a jet fighter make what looked to be a strafing run on something on the desert floor near Cornville. These two incidents on the same evening occurred several minutes apart and were approximately eight linear miles from each other.

The witnesses of these two separate events do not know each other. The following excerpt is from a transcript of a taped phone interview I had with the ex-Vietnam pilot:

"The jets came from the north straight at me. They were so close together that the red running lights looked like one. They made a breaking turn to the east, and when they climbed higher I saw the two running lights. Then I knew that it was two jets. On the upward climb one of the jets turned off its lights. That's what they do when they start an attack; the wing man keeps his lights on while the lead plane turns its lights off and comes down. That way you can't tell which is doing what. After the attack is made, the plane making the run turns its lights back on. And that's exactly what happened. It looked like they were attacking a stationary object on the ground. I saw that and thought, this is all so bizarre — what the hell is going on here? They were going after something about a half-mile away from me. I could hear the engines but I didn't hear any cannon fire and I didn't see any rockets or tracers."

(*Author's note:* Tracers are flaming bullets, used to see the path of the bullets. This does not rule out that the jets shot at something. If the wind were blowing away from the witness, the plane's guns may not have been heard easily. Also, the jets may have been photographing something. Another possibility is that one or both of them may have been firing a particle-beam weapon. Military sources say that it is 99% certain that some U.S. and Russian jet fighters are now equipped with beam-type weapons instead of machine guns and rockets.)

On July 28, my close friends and associates, Claudia and Mark, interviewed a very nervous Cottonwood man who says he remembers being abducted by a UFO during the early part of July in Sycamore Canyon. He explained how he was taken into a UFO and was placed naked on an operating table. On the table next to him was a woman, also nude. She seemed to be under some sort of anesthesia. What alarmed him most was that he watched a "praying mantis-like machine" probe with a pointed device at many areas of her body. Then the machine moved toward him, and his memory failed him at that point.

On the evening of July 31, it was arranged for Ray (whose experience is related earlier in this chapter) to be hypnotized by a psychiatrist. Ray had an experience in Sycamore Canyon where he thought he had missing time. I was present with seven others at the session conducted by Carlos Warter, M.D., of Sedona. Dr. Warter is an expert in this particular field. We felt fortunate to have a competent professional doing the hypnosis session, as these types of matters must be handled by those who know what they are doing.

The session itself lasted for 45 minutes, and during this time the only people present in the room were Dr. Warter, Ray and a fellow who was recording the session with a tripod-mounted camcorder. While the session was in progress, the rest of us went outside to wait on Dr. Warter's wooden deck, which affords views of Soldiers Pass and an expansive area of sky. While the others were talking, I found a comfortable spot and lay down on the deck to watch a sky full of storm clouds. Moments later I experienced one of the most dramatic UFO sightings I have ever had.

Lying there with my head propped up on a rubber ball and absent-mindedly listening to the others' discussion, my eyes focused on an object that looked like the landing lights of a small airplane — very common here, as the local airport was only about a mile away. Listening to the others, I watched this light, not seeing anything unusual about it. Then suddenly the light stretched out like one might pull on a ball of taffy, and this funnel-shaped light bent upward as I watched, in a 30- or 40-degree angle. There was a pause of about two seconds, then a point of white light streaked off into space at a fantastic speed. This light or craft was about the same size and brightness as a large earth satellite. I have no idea what its actual size was. It took a few moments for me to realize what I had just seen. None of the others could have seen it because I was the only one facing in that direction. Later I told Dr. Warter about it. He didn't seem to think it was such a big deal, and he told me about some of his and others' sightings from the same deck. My sighting was apparently somewhat puny beside some of the things others had seen from there.

The hypnosis session had been completed, so we all gathered inside to see what was on the videotape. The following are excerpts from it. You will notice that Ray's information largely agrees with the channeled information (which I have now read) to follow in a few pages.

Ray is at this point deep in hypnosis and Dr. Warter has begun to ask him questions:

Walk forward into that canyon [Sycamore] and describe out loud the sensations, feelings and perceptions that come into your mind.

I see ... like a glass ... in the air. I am walking, walking ... (*stops*).

Look through this thing in the air.

I see, I see ... a triangle. I'm walking, walking ... in the canyon. But I'm not in the canyon.

Where are you?

(*Ray becomes distressed.*) I'm inside something!

Can you describe it? There is no need to be afraid. There is no need to be afraid now, since you are watching your own memories. Just walk into that form and describe what took place, knowing that you are safe. You are safe right here, right now.

(*Still nervous, now breathing heavily.*) I am walking through this glaze, this mirror ... it's clear ... and ... I see my body below me and I see the canyon walls! I am rising ... looking.

Where are you?

I'm above the walls of the canyon. I feel something pull me up!

What is pulling you up?

This light ... light ... bright light. Pulling.

Please continue. Where are you now?

I can't! I can't! (*He shows great fear.*)

Remove all imprints of negativity of this experience. Go to the event objectively now. Look. Move on. You are safe.

(*Ray is mumbling, breathing harder.*)

You are doing very well. Please describe it.

I saw something. I saw a white head! (*Ray is speaking low, as if he doesn't want to be heard.*)

A white head? Say that louder, please.

A white head! I saw a white, oval head! (*Ray is terrified now, panting and twitching as he speaks.*) There's more than one!

What happened?

A light. I just see this bright light! And now I see two colors in it, a white color and a darker color. There's this light! A light right there — above me! Right above me!

Where are the oval heads?

To … to my! … to my …! (*He is again terrified.*)

Yes. Identify them. You are safe now.

Gray. Gray bodies! Gray bodies! Yes … they … (*He stops.*)

Do they communicate?

Behind them is a light — a light. A white light. There is a yellow light in front of me.

Do you receive any communication from them? What do they want?

(*Without hesitation.*) They want something from me.

Can you identify precisely what happened?

No, it's blocked. They want … they are just looking at me.

Are you being touched?

No.

Move forward in the experience now to what happened sequentially after that. It's safe to look.

The eyes, no! (*He changes to a calm tone of voice.*) Feel peace. I feel fine now.

Were you probed?

I think so … yes.

Do you know the purpose of the probe?

For reproduction. There is something I have in my right knee. They are probing my right knee.

Are you in contact with them now? If you want to, do so.

(*No response.*)

Where in your body or your mind is your contact with them?

(*Long pause.*) It's right here. (*He points with his left hand.*) In my left temple.

The session continued for another half-hour. Ray said that there was a monitoring implant in his left temple. He remembers being on a sort of surgical table with a revolving white light off to his right. The aliens probed his knee with a device like a long needle. Ray said that there was no pain with the procedure. When asked what the aliens' intention on Earth was, he answered that they were "exploring without being known." They are curious about us. He said that there was an erosion problem with their planet and ours, and they are pressured in some way. They told him they are here to protect us and to guard against a mass hysteria of humanity. There is evidently some sort of a warlike conflict going on between certain alien groups. Also, "something was getting ready to break and we would be educated to outside life soon." The session basically ended at that point.

On July 29, a fire broke out on top of Secret Mountain. The U.S. Forest Service says that it was caused by lightning, but no one I've talked to can remember any lightning activity that day. The fire burned for five days before an attempt was made to put it out. On Tuesday, August 2, fire crews were mobilized to fight the fire. Half of these crews came from New Mexico, as evidently Arizona crews were tied up fighting other Arizona fires. When the fire first began, helicopters were seen above Secret Mountain playing searchlights around the fire — an odd fire-fighting technique, as fire-fighting helicopters and planes almost never fly at night because of the danger.

In the early stages of the fire, yellow smoke was occasionally seen billowing up from the mountain. Wood smoke is usually black, gray or white. There are no man-made structures on Secret Mountain except the remains of a cowboy-era log cabin on the northwest side of the mountain. Near the exact spot and time the fire started, a UFO was seen flying low over Secret Mountain. The fire, named the "Lost Fire" [the fire supposedly started on Lost Mountain but an eyewitness account puts it on Secret Mountain], burned for ten days. At one point after about seven days, the fire got out of control and jumped over onto the Colorado Plateau. It had burned over 1800 acres of pine and elm forest before it was stopped by rain late on August 8.

At the height of the blaze, from Sedona Secret Mountain looked like an erupting volcano. Flames could be seen at night from as far away as 50 miles. From the time the fire began on Secret Mountain (July 29), all UFO, jet fighter and military helicopter activity has ceased in the area. Today is August 8. There has not been one report of a jet fighter, military helicopter or UFO activity anywhere in this area — after two months of almost constant activity and sightings. This seems rather curious.

In many writings I have done over the past four years, I have been saying that something extraordinary must be centered or based on Secret Mountain, due to a multitude of reports of very strange military and paranormal activity in that area. One wonders if whatever might have been there in the past has now been destroyed.

Because of the many unusual and paranormal events/sightings that occurred during the general period around Memorial Day weekend, one can speculate that there is in this area something that both the U.S. government and extraterrestrials are extremely interested in. Could it be, for example, an underground base of some sort? Or perhaps an interdimensional base in the same physical location as Secret Mountain and/or House Mountain? Could it even be an interdimensional portal or a doorway to who-knows-what-or-where?

From the information I have accumulated I would have to conclude that during that general time period of May 28–30, 1994, a flying craft of extreme military sensitivity crashed, landed or was shot down in one of two locations. One location would be the south slope area of House Mountain. The second location would likely be in the zone between Red Canyon and Highway 89A — an area of ten square miles.

UFO Researcher Witnesses Battle in the Sky

August 26, 1994

Before I go into the UFO incident that is the point of this article, I want to mention that at the time of this writing, August 26, 1994, I have experienced four UFO sightings in twenty-one days. However, this most recent experience was, to put it mildly, more dramatic than the first three. The first and second occurred as I was giving an outdoor UFO talk to fifteen people; a UFO flew toward us. As it got closer it simply blinked out. There was a similar sighting later on in the evening. The third sighting took place as Sedona resident Dr. Carlos Warter was hypnotically regressing a Sedona resident who had recently been abducted. I watched from outside on Dr. Warter's back deck as a ball of white light, which I thought at first was an airplane's landing lights, exploded into a far larger light. For several seconds the expanded light from this object actually bent upward as it turned and then streaked off into space.

In discussing the fourth sighting, I will mention, for credibility purposes, that two other adult witnesses four miles from where I was saw the same things I did but from an entirely different vantage point. On the day of this incident, August 23, I had been feeling low on energy and tremendously out of sorts. I just couldn't get up to speed all day. I had been invited to go on a hike at 6:00PM with a group of friends. I opted not to go, which is very unlike me. Instead, I decided to sleep in my van out in the canyons that night and went out early to a favorite campsite. If I had not declined the hike, I would not have had the experience that night.

It got dark about 7:45PM and as it grew darker I noticed that more jet aircraft than usual were flying around in the night sky. A major east/west air route crosses over Sedona, so commercial jet traffic here is common. I noticed that night, though, that some of these high-flying jets were nowhere near the usual commercial air corridors. As the minutes passed and it got progressively darker. (There was an almost-full moon that night, but it didn't rise until 9:00PM.) I couldn't help noticing that jets were becoming more and more numerous. Then formations of jet fighters began showing up and were criss-crossing the cloudless, completely clear night sky in differing directions and at differing altitudes. There were jets in ones, twos, threes and fives flying within sight of my position, which was on a high overlook near the road to Vultee Arch. I could see for many miles. I estimated that there were at least twenty military jet aircraft of jet-fighter to commercial-airliner size, flying at altitudes of 7,000 to 20,000 feet. My campsite elevation was about 4,600 feet.

Then things really got interesting and I ended up staying up the entire night, as did the Loy Butte witnesses who were four miles to the west of me. At 8:35PM two fighters flying in formation in the northeast at about 10,000 feet were fired at from the southeast. The "shot" came from below the jets and looked very much like a meteorite, but this went up, not down. Minutes later two other jet fighters were making a wide banking turn at about 8,000 feet near Secret Canyon. These two jets were fired at by something I could not see above and to the northwest. In both cases the jets did not change course or take any defensive or offensive action that I could see. The same applied to all the other jets. They all just seemed to be waiting and watching something. Those shots, or whatever they were, seemed to me to be warnings, like firing a shot over the bow of a ship. Keep in mind that the crews of these jet aircraft, which could have included as many as one hundred pilots and navigators or more, obviously knew in detail what was going on that night.

What I witnessed that night is of inestimable significance to us commoners, but we are being kept in the dark by our own countrymen. Why? Is government fear of panic and retribution that great? I doubt it. I think there is more to it than that. And if these pilots and crews were briefed on what was going on, there are probably a thousand more who are in on this thing, including the entire subject of aliens and UFOs in general.

At 8:40PM, as I was intently watching jets, I was looking northeast. I turned to look to the west and there, at about 8,000 feet, was an object of tremendous size flying from west to east. It was moving at about 200 mph and made no sound at all. This object, or craft, had the general pattern of a round cluster of white lights and several red lights. All of these lights moved in perfect unison across the clear night sky. They seemed to be attached to a huge, dark craft the size and shape of which I could not determine even in bright moonlight. In a state of absolute awe, I watched the huge object fly to the north of Capitol Butte and then right over the center of Sedona. I asked numerous local residents if they had seen anything unusual in the sky that night and most replied that they had been watching television.

I turned to look to the far west from where the craft had come. There, brightly illuminated by moonlight on the north side of Secret Mountain, was a billowing, towering column of white smoke about 1,000 feet high and approximately 500 feet wide. Smoke at the base of this growing column was caught in a breeze and was drifting across the top of Secret Mountain to the south for over half a mile. I did not see a flash and did not hear an explosion, but the column of white smoke must have been connected with the strange craft with red and white lights that had just passed over Secret Mountain.

Several weeks prior to this August 23rd incident there had been a forest fire on Secret Mountain that had burned for ten days and had charred over 2,000 acres of Ponderosa pine and scrub oak forest. The fire is of extremely suspicious origin and circumstance. Jet fighters, helicopters and UFOs figure strongly in this event. It took about an hour for the smoke from the explosion (or implosion) to disperse.

I was so engrossed in and fascinated by what I was watching that I never even gave a thought to the camera and audio recording equipment I had sitting in a case several feet away, prepared for just such an event. The jets gradually thinned out and by 10:00PM only an occasional airliner was flying overhead. Hours passed like minutes that night. And then

**Photo of UFOs on the same night the smoke column was seen.
See the photo/drawing on the opposite page.**

suddenly, at 10:52PM, an incredible sphere of blazing chrome-white light descended out of the sky in the west, high over Secret Mountain. This sphere became brighter and brighter as it descended. It slowed, and as it did it became dimmer and dimmer and then blinked out entirely exactly in the center of where the towering pillar of white smoke had been over Secret Mountain. If this light had landed it would have come down on the exact center, the "ground zero," of the mysterious explosion of a few hours earlier.

Then, at 11:15PM, through my binoculars I watched an aircraft with a red and a green light and a white strobe light fly at slow speed north to south over the same area of the earlier smoke pillar on Secret Mountain. At 11:25PM a sphere of chrome-white light identical to the one I saw a half-hour earlier flew very slowly, south to north, on the same flight path the aircraft had taken.

I finally remembered the camera and thoroughly chastised myself for being so stupid and negligent, but better late than never, I thought.

Drawing of area where smoke column was seen.

So I put the camera, a Minolta X-370 SLR with 1600-speed film, in a spot where I could grab it in an instant. Feeling increasingly drowsy and thinking that the action was probably over, I lay down on the bed in my camper but kept my eyes on Secret Mountain through the back windows. I began dozing off and finally fell asleep.

Some minutes later my eyes snapped open almost automatically. I looked at Maroon Mountain, which is just to the north side of Secret Mountain. Two blazing spheres of chrome-white lights skimmed across the top of Maroon Mountain and flew in a graceful curving formation straight in my direction.

In one electrified instant I grabbed the camera and stumbled out of the van barefoot and dressed only in a pair of hiking shorts. I was overwhelmed with fear and fascination as the lights came rapidly closer. The beauty of those chrome-white lights is impossible to describe accurately. I have never seen anything like it. They came closer and closer and then stopped and hovered a short distance from where I stood. They began to dim rapidly and I snapped a photo. The camera jammed. A top-of-the-line

Minolta that has never given me a bit of trouble jammed as two UFOs hovered right in front of me, as if giving me a perfect shot. My heart sank and I remember thinking that the whole thing was right out of a Steven Spielberg movie. A scriptwriter couldn't have done it better than this.

Then the lights blinked out. "They" were right there, sitting out there in the dark, but I could not see them. I looked all around, behind, above, both sides. I could not see them but I knew they were there. And what were they going to do? I thought, "This is it — and no witnesses." I took up my note pad and quickly scribbled in large letters this message: "12:10AM two brilliant balls of light coming straight in my direction — flew over Maroon Mountain." If I disappeared for a while or for good, at least there would be a note. The Travis Walton experience was heavy on my mind in those moments.

The next day, while fiddling with the camera, I discovered that a thin plastic ring liner just behind the lens opening had come loose and had gotten stuck in the mirror of the camera, jamming the mirror in the open position, blocking the viewfinder and locking the shutter. As it turns out, the photo I took came out anyway, although it was taken at a time when the lights were a tiny fraction of their flying brightness. But at least it was something.

At that point, I got fully dressed and prepared to stay up the rest of the night. There was no way I was going to try to sleep. Then things took a different, even stranger turn. At 12:30AM a carload of drunken Mexicans pulled off the road several hundred yards away and opened the car doors so that everything within two miles could hear trumpets and accordion music blasting from their car stereo. They must have had speakers three feet high in that car. This sort of thing normally infuriates me, but that night I welcomed the company and noise. They were drinking and shouting until 4:00AM. Maybe the UFO will get them instead, I thought. The loud music woke a man sleeping in a late-model white Jeep Cherokee between me and the Mexicans. He started the motor, turned on the headlights and then drove around the desert erratically for ten minutes. He seemed to find a better spot four or five times before he finally just drove away in the direction of Sedona. Extremely odd behavior, it seemed.

At almost the same time the UFOs had blinked out and the Mexicans had arrived, I had heard a tremendous crashing in the brush to my left about 150 feet away. The crashing continued steadily but the music was so loud it almost drowned out the crashing and snapping sounds in the dry piñon pine and manzanita. Those of us who spend a lot of time in the high desert know how tough manzanita bushes are. The one- to two-inch trunks and limbs are like iron and when the limbs break they leave jagged edges.

Three things had begun happening almost simultaneously: the Mexicans, the white Jeep and the crashing in the brush. At about 12:45AM I realized that whatever was in the brushy forest was of extreme weight. It sounded like three or four thousand-pound steers, all plowing through heavy brush. That's what cattle do. If they are going somewhere, they go through things, not around them. But then I remembered that there hadn't been any cattle in that particular area for a long time. As I listened to the crashing slowly moving away from me I realized that something was highly out of the ordinary. There was too much crashing too continuously. A cow would stop and graze or moo or something, but there was just this steady, linear, heavy crashing of brush, with the sounds receding from where I was.

I stood there wondering why in the hell it's always me who sees this stuff and has these kinds of experiences. I have four, soon to be five, widely distributed books full of these types of occurrences. Many of these unusual incidents and experiences were witnessed by at least one other adult individual.

I became so engrossed by whatever was making the crashing sounds that for a while I completely forgot about the UFOs. With my big six-volt flashlight I walked across a wide, sandy clearing to the area where I had first heard the crashing sounds. I cautiously made my way a short distance into the pines and manzanitas. Although the moon was directly overhead and bright, I unavoidably stepped on some twigs I did not see. The crashing sounds, about 100 yards away at that point, stopped. Whatever it was, it was now watching me. I was on a higher ridge and the tallest pines below were up to ten feet high but sparse enough so that I should have been able to see what it was that was doing the crashing. I turned on the powerful flashlight and shone the beam all around down below in the area where I had last heard brush snapping. I couldn't see anything out of the ordinary.

In the unlikely event it was deer, the only nondomestic animal heavy enough to perhaps make such sounds, they would get curious and look at the light and I would see their shining eyes reflected. But I saw no eyes and no cow or deer silhouette and I heard no sound. I switched the light off and reasoned that it just had to be cattle. As I walked away the heavy crashing of brush slowly and cautiously resumed and then slowly faded away to the southwest.

I went back to the van and waited up the rest of the night. Nothing else of an unusual nature happened that night.

At first light I searched the area of the crashing brush sounds. In the dry dusty soil there were no fresh tracks of any kind except for those of one medium-sized deer, which would have weighed no more than 100 pounds. During the night the deer had passed through the gully nonstop on its way somewhere. It was not the maker of the sounds. What made the crashing noises? I have not the slightest idea what it was. The next day I learned that a local rancher has had this same experience several times near his ranch.

As a result of what I (and two others) saw that Tuesday night, August 23, 1994, my life has not been and never again will be the same. We all might take a more serious view of UFO activities, particularly as they now concern and involve all of us. I think too many people still put UFOs into the entertainment category.

. . .

Just after completing the above, I learned that on Tuesday, August 16, 1994, at 8:40PM, two prominent Sedona business owners had watched the same huge white-and-red-lit object I had seen on Tuesday, August 23. In this sighting the craft flew north to south over Sedona at a very high speed and was being chased, unsuccessfully, by two jet fighters.

At 10:00PM, Thursday, August 25, 1994, I was visiting at a friend's house in the Quail Hollow subdivision. Suddenly the house, brand new and large, began to vibrate violently. It took us a few seconds to realize that there were helicopters over the roof of the house. The helicopters were moving fast. We grabbed a pair of binoculars and ran out onto the back deck. The moon was just rising in the northeast and it silhouetted the helicopters perfectly. With the binoculars, we got a good look at them. They were flying at roof-top height. The lead helicopter had one red light underneath, but the two following helicopters were completely dark — no lights on at all. FAA-approved?

We later discussed the fact that it seemed as though they were chasing something, but we didn't see what it might have been. As it turns out, a group of local witnesses saw what the military helicopters were indeed chasing. These people were at Posse Grounds Park. This is high ground that overlooks most of Sedona. They heard the helicopters coming from the south and turned to look in that direction. Two spheres of blue light flew past them at high speed about 100 feet above the ground. The lights were about a foot in diameter and might have been attached to a larger, darker object. The lights were about a quarter of a mile ahead of the helicopters.

The balls of blue light went across the city of Sedona and up Schnebly Hill. Schnebly Hill is actually a wide, steep canyon. The lights made a U-turn halfway up Schnebly Hill and then disappeared to the east. The helicopters (it's not known what model they were) continued straight up Oak Creek Canyon and then over the 6,000-foot Mogollon Rim above Sedona. This whole incident lasted for no more than 60 to 90 seconds.

September 20, 1994

I want to thank the many readers who have written and expressed great interest and support in my writing about UFOs, aliens and the paranormal. It can be, and often is, an infernally frustrating business in many ways. And thank you too, for all the interesting personal experiences you have sent to me.

Sedona really is, in a paranormal sense, an extraordinary and unusual place. Sedona is likely a neutral zone between time and dimensions, a portal area that allows all sorts of things to enter — or to go back and forth. This includes numerous varieties of flying crafts and their crews. I think it also includes a few lower, questionably intelligent creatures that have an ability to materialize and dematerialize in the general Sedona area. In the last four months there has been almost continuous supernormal activity, some of which is difficult to rationalize with conventional terminology. I am presently involved in an investigation, very tangible, that is in the purest sense supernormal or supernatural. It is in no way negative. It probably has little to do with UFOs or UFO aliens. To protect identities and locations I am not going to be more specific. This activity, from what I've seen, falls, directly into the realms of the extreme paranormal. I hope to get four or five or more good photographs for my research.

On September 12 about 8:30PM I witnessed something quite unusual, and I wasn't the only one. A Sedona woman saw the same objects that I did, but from a different, and apparently better, vantage point. She was a mile or so east of me, which gave her a clearer view than I had. As astonishing as this sighting was, no one else seems to have observed it.

As I was gazing toward the north at the night sky, I caught a glimpse of odd lights heading in my direction. I lost sight of them, but I mentally plotted their trajectory and watched where they should appear. To my amazement, a cluster of red-and-white lights appeared, and seconds later a second cluster appeared several hundred yards behind the first. These two clusters had the general shape of a triangle and silently circled the city of Sedona three times at an altitude of about 3000 feet. On the second and third passes I snapped a half-dozen photos, one of which is printed below.

There has been enough UFO and other unusual activity in the Sedona area in the past four months to give me fuel for a long-term investigation. I received the following letter in the mail the other day, which typifies what has been transpiring here lately. Without a doubt Sedona is again the world's hot spot for UFO activity. The letter follows, and I thank Dana for sending it.

Dear Tom,

Greetings! Let me first express my appreciation for the thorough and informative research you have done, as evidenced by your books, which I have found to be very compelling, exciting and thought-provoking.

I wanted to share a mysterious experience/sighting I had on the night of Wednesday, August 31st. I figure you must have had other reports regarding the same occurrence and probably have an idea of what actually took place. I for one am baffled, and if my report can simply serve to reinforce or duplicate someone else's report, then my mission is accomplished.

Between 7:45PM and 8:00PM, on the night of August 31st, I was driving east out Jacks Canyon Road from the Village of Oak Creek. The sun had already disappeared behind the horizon to the west, and the sky was getting dark. As I looked out my front car window in a northeastern direction, I noticed a strange pinkish cloud above and beyond Lee Mountain. I could not figure out how this cloud was illuminated, as the sky was getting too dark and the other clouds over the western horizon weren't getting any light from the setting sun. Suddenly I saw this pink cloud light up (from within or below) in a bright yellow flash that lasted perhaps a full second or two, then faded. There was no lightning activity in the night sky at all. I pulled over and continued my observation out of the car.

My first thought was that something had exploded or crashed on the ground. However, approximately 30 seconds later, this flash of light occurred again and again and again in about 30-second intervals for about 30 minutes! Within 15 minutes of my first sighting of this event, in the sky over this area (approximately 10 miles from my position) I counted eight flying craft, which I suspected were helicopters because of the stationary positions the red and white lights were assuming in the night sky. I then noticed two pairs of red and white lights in formation flying from the area in my direction, banking to circle and return to the area of activity. These lights looked like wing-tip lights on two jet aircraft surveying the scene.

I thought that I might get to a closer vantage point if I drove out to Interstate 17 and headed north toward Flagstaff to the overlook area. This I proceeded to do, and approximately 25 minutes later I was there, only to discover no more aircraft in the sky. The flashing light had apparently moved to a position farther northeast of my position, northeast of Stoneman Lake. I returned home not knowing any more about this event.

What Dana probably should have done, if possible, was pull off the road and from there watch the activity over Lee Mountain. I don't know how many times I have driven farther in an effort to find a better vantage point only to find the object, or objects, gone when I got closer. Sometimes you have to grab the opportunity as it is — because often it may only last seconds, or minutes at best. A pair of binoculars and even an inexpensive point-and-shoot camera carried in the car is a great asset in an active UFO area. Often a distant object on a three-by-five 200 or 400 ASA supermarket photo print can be enlarged with stunning results. High-speed film does not usually work well because high-speed (1000 ASA or above) is just too grainy for good enlargements.

I have recently watched large and small aircraft change running lights into different patterns in a seeming effort to look like a UFO or something else. Why? I have also seen what I think was a huge UFO trying to look like a very large jet aircraft. The craft, however, made no sound whatsoever. A number of people have seen that around here. I have also seen jet fighters flying in a manner that to me strongly suggested they were expecting or were ready for an attack. An attack by whom or what in U.S. airspace?

A week ago, on the night of September 13, during a wild series of UFO sightings, I saw what looked to be a small, probably twin-engine plane coming toward me at a low altitude. With only the naked eye it simply looked like a small plane making an approach to the Sedona airport with its landing lights on. But when I picked up my binoculars and looked at it, it was a different sight altogether. In the middle, on the underside of the plane, was a red, flashing strobe light. To the right and left of the strobe and what would be the middle of a light plane's wings, were two bright landing lights. But on the outer edge of each wing was a light that slowly pulsed with such a blazing brightness that at the peak of each pulse all you could see was the red strobe and a small inner portion of the "landing lights." It then turned east and flew right over Sedona. A UFO trying to look like a plane or a plane trying to look like a UFO? Whatever it was, it wasn't normal.

To make matters even more interesting, from the same general direction that the "twin-engine plane" approached, appeared two moving red lights in the distance. These lights were at first a pinpoint, but as they moved closer I got a clear look at them through my binoculars. These two lights, or spheres, were a deep crimson red and pulsed at intervals of about three seconds. They would each pulse separately: a long bright pulse, a diminishing brightness, a three-second or so pause and then the same long bright pulse lasting about five seconds.

I would estimate the diameter of each sphere at approximately two feet. They may have been much smaller or much larger, because I had no frame of reference such as trees or a mountaintop. These two lights flew in tandem and pulsed at exactly the same rate, although separately, and were moving at a speed of what I would judge to be between 80–100 mph. The two objects stayed close to each other, but slightly altered their relative position to one another as they flew, and disappeared behind a low mountain to the east.

At about that same time, west of Sedona a number of witnesses saw two white glowing UFOs followed at a distance by a jet fighter. One of the UFOs made a sharp reverse turn and headed straight for the fighter as if it were playing chicken with the fighter. Just before it would have hit the fighter the UFO made an abrupt 90-degree turn to the east and disappeared. This sort of thing, or something similar, has been seen a number of times around here. It almost seems like tempers are getting a bit short.

February 1993

As I mentioned in last month's column, doing paranormal research is a fascinating business because I never know what I'm going to run across. Occasionally I meet someone who has had a Yeti, Sasquatch or Bigfoot experience. There seems to be four or five distinctly different type of these creatures; often some are extremely intelligent.

I recently talked briefly with a man who had a marvelously interesting Bigfoot experience. It seems that this fellow had his experience in a remote area of the Utah Canyonlands while making his living as a wilderness guide in the La Salle Mountains where he was living in a cabin. One day he heard an odd commotion on the deck of his cabin. Since the area has a lot of black bears, he thought a bear had come up on the deck. He saw something furry moving around and thought a bear had smelled his cooler, which was filled with food — bears love coolers filled with food. He made some loud noises with pots and pans and yelled loudly at the bear. But the creature did not run away like a normal bear. I have chased a few black bears myself and they usually behave like a dog in someone else's backyard; I know how fearful most bears are of humans.

The man started for the door to the deck, and as he did, he saw that the creature was not a bear but a fur-covered human-like creature standing on two legs and looking at him. He said it was about six feet five inches in height, weighed around 230 pounds and was extremely muscular. As the "Bigfoot" saw the man coming, it leaped off the deck and bounded across a wide clearing in three strides — and was out of sight.

What made the encounter even more remarkable is that the creature had placed the heavy cooler against the door so the man could not get out to the deck quickly. The only item that was missing from the cooler was a block of butter; nothing else was disturbed. The creature could have easily taken the whole cooler but didn't. It wanted only the butter, so that was all it took. These are not, as the man pointed out, the actions of a dumb or greedy animal. This gentleman was articulate and intelligent, as are most people I meet who have had unexpected paranormal encounters. Just normal everyday people, as is the man in this next incident.

A UFO Incident

I debated with myself for weeks whether or not to relate this incident. One of the primary reasons for my reluctance is that I was injured quite severely during the course of my involvement in this story and went to the hospital for a short stay. Being injured may or may not have anything to do with this, but it is interesting that a number of UFO researchers I know of were hurt, or even killed during a specific investigation and/or had part or all of their records and property mysteriously destroyed. I have learned that this is not a game. I have researched hundreds of UFO or alien-related incidents, and I think this one bothers me more than any of the others of a highly alien nature. I'm not really sure why this particular incident bothers me so much, because there are many more I have run across that are far more bizarre than this one. It may be, I suppose, that on some dim level I have had a similar experience. Some of this story I have omitted for personal reasons.

In the 1950s outside of Birmingham, Alabama, a man who travels a lot in his job was followed in the early morning hours by a large, blazing-bright UFO. He was driving on a major highway and the UFO may have paced his car for as long as three hours. The UFO was front-page news the next day in Alabama because a lot of people saw it. After this man's (I'll call him Mr. Bensen) experience, all sorts of things began to be different in his life and his family's life. Mr. Bensen seemed to be a bit different after the sighting and his income strangely increased far above the norm for a man in his profession. Several months after the initial incident a house near the Bensens was sold, and the new occupants, along with strangers, were seen coming and going at odd hours of the day and night. In short, there was a lot of abnormal activity at this house, and this was in the days before the onslaught of drug dealers.

Black cars frequented this neighborhood and men dressed all in black would come to the door of the Bensen house. They would ask odd questions and leave. (Men-in-Black, known as MIB in the UFO business, black limousines and black helicopters were once very common and were always directly related to UFO incidents.) Because the newspaper had published Mr. Bensen's name, there were also many UFO-related phone calls, some the usual crank type. After one very unusual call, Mr. Bensen ordered the family never to speak of the incident again.

Then, to cap the whole episode, very late one night another family member heard Mr. Bensen quietly leave his bedroom and walk down the hall. The other family member silently followed Mr. Bensen into the living room, the latter unaware he was being watched. Bensen stopped in front of the fireplace, looked up, and a round penlight-type light appeared on his face. The only problem was that there was no originating source for the light — only the round light on his face. He seemed to be in a semi-trance and was making silent face and head gestures as if he were talking to someone. This went on for awhile and then the light lifted off Mr. Bensen's face, descended downward, turned and then disappeared up the chimney. Mr. Bensen died several days later.

Many years after Bensen's death, the family member who had observed that incident very reluctantly told a third family member. It was then that the third member admitted he had seen the same occurrence on a number of occasions, but had never spoken of it to the rest of the family. This third family member (who is in a high government position) said he would not, and could not, discuss the incident further. Period. One has to wonder why he did not want to discuss it further. What did he know that he did not want to talk about?

As I've said on many occasions before, I think there is something out there that is probably beyond our ability to fully comprehend. Something probably only a handful of Earth humans know about. It is not of a particularly spiritual nature, and is no doubt entirely alien in the way it interacts with our system. In my research, I run across such a probability time and time again. I think the novelist Louis L'Amour put it best when he said, "If there are other worlds parallel to ours, are all of the doors closed? Or does one, here or there, stand ajar?"

March 1993

It seems almost everything happens to me in bunches. For instance, lately I have been running across the Anasazi, right and left. The Anasazi were an ancient tribe of Indians who long ago lived in harmony and peace in the American Southwest for a thousand or more years. Although I am fairly well versed in Indian history, the Anasazi have not been one of my major interests. But this story is different — very different.

A lot of mystery still surrounds the Anasazi. They were a decidedly advanced civilization. In areas of cultural achievement (art, astronomy, architecture) and in their pursuits of things of an intellectual and spiritual nature, they were far ahead of most early North American civilizations. Anthropologists and archeologists are still trying to understand the Anasazi. It is evident that some of the Anasazi merged with other tribes and some splinter groups became what we now know of as the Hopi, Zuni and Pueblo tribes. But the fact remains that a large part of the Anasazi nation simply vanished. UFO aliens may have played a major role in that disappearance.

The Anasazi (the Navaho word for "ancient ones") made their home in the Four Corners border area of Utah, Colorado, Arizona (including Sedona) and New Mexico. Many thousands of Anasazi once lived in this area.

**Cliff Palace, one of many Anasazi ruins.
Mesa Verde National Park.**

In its heyday, the Anasazi had a thriving and efficient civilization. The "capitol" of the Anasazi nation was located at Chaco Canyon in what is now northwest New Mexico. The Chaco Canyon civic complex was the hub of commerce and social activity for the Anasazi. There were over 400 miles of roadways leading out of Chaco Canyon to over one hundred out-lying Anasazi townships. I've seen enhanced satellite photos of the Anasazi road network and it looks very much like the mysterious lines at Nazca in Peru. Pueblo Bonito still stands in Chaco Canyon. It is of Anasazi architecture, is five stories tall and has over 700 rooms. These were not a primitive people. Around the year 1125 A.D., things began to go wrong for the Anasazi. Their population was becoming too large, they had worn out their usable crop land by overplanting and they had cut down most of their forests for firewood and construction material. (Sound familiar?)

Then, at the height of their problems, it is evident that the entire population of their governmental center at Chaco Canyon simply vanished! This seems to have thrown the remaining Anasazi into turmoil and panic. They abandoned their mesa-top and flatland pueblos and began construction of new dwellings, often in almost inaccessible lofty recesses on perpendicular cliff walls. These apartment-like cliff houses were just as often built deep in defendable cave-like alcoves. These cave fortresses are still in an excellent state of preservation in Mesa Verde National Park in southeast Colorado. Mesa Verde is a fascinating study of Anasazi life and Anasazi fortress architecture. A single structure often accommodated a hundred or more Anasazi men, women and children. But — the question remains that no one can answer — what were the Anasazi preparing to defend against? (Around the world there are parallels to the disappearance of the Chaco Canyon Anasazi, such as the populations of Machu Picchu in Peru, Angkor Wat in Cambodia, Tiahuanaco on Lake Titicaca in Bolivia and at least a dozen other cities and civilizations in the times of recorded history. All of the human inhabitants seem to have simply vanished.)

There are hundreds of Anasazi ruins in the Four Corners area that were constructed with the obvious intent of defense — but again, who was the enemy? There has never been evidence found of sieges or of organized, largescale attacks on the Anasazi cliff houses. This time period was long before the Navaho, Apache or Caucasian incursions. The Hopis, it has been determined, are direct descendants of the Anasazi. The Hopis have a legend that speaks of the "Ant People." The Ant People are godlike beings who live underground and who will return at some point in the future and take the Hopis with them at a time of dramatic Earth change. The Hopis will return to the surface when the Earth is again safe and habitable. Could the Hopi legend be directly attributed to what might have happened concerning the disappearance of the elite of the Anasazi civilization at Chaco Canyon? Did the remaining Anasazi for some reason, perhaps out of ignorance, fear the Ant People and the fiery ships they might have traveled in? Hence, the hard-to-get-to locations where they constructed their cliff houses.

Compare the Ant People with present-day descriptions of encountered aliens, particularly those who have come to be known as "The Greys." The similarity is unmistakable. Did the Ant People take the entire Chacoan population with them to a safer place? About the time of the disappearance of the Chaco Canyon population, a 24-year drought devastated the remaining Anasazis. As a result, after about the year 1300, the Anasazi Nation had totally disintegrated. Some of the Anasazi then moved to the Rio Grande Valley in New Mexico and to several other locations. Had the Ant People been in the Chaco Canyon area all along — perhaps for millennia before the arrival of the Indians? Did the Ant People assume, possibly out of kindness, stewardship over the burgeoning peaceful Anasazi population?

Hopi legend also speaks of the God Maasaw who comes in a fiery ball of blue light. The last appearance of Maasaw was evidently in the early 1940s. Hopi legend says that anyone who looks at one of these Maasaw entities quickly falls unconscious — identical to modern alien-human encounters. Unconsciousness occurs in about 50 percent of present-day encounters.)

The Four Corners area has long been a hot spot for UFO/alien activity. It's a sparsely populated, mostly desert region. Rumors and evidence of UFO activity and underground bases are almost constant in this general area. Nearby are Dulse, New Mexico, where there is supposedly a huge underground alien base, Roswell and Corona, New Mexico, and the Plains of San Augustin where there is strong evidence of two major UFO crashes in 1947–48. A UFO may have crashed in Aztec, N.M., in the 1970s — again, strong evidence. Sedona has been a UFO hot spot since the 1920s.

The great question remains: where did the Chaco Canyon Anasazi go? If, by chance, they went to an alien world, underground, or to another dimension, or whatever, could it be they are now coming back to the Southwest for some, unknown to us, essential or highly spiritual reason? The reason I mention this is that so many people who come to the Southwest (particularly to Sedona) often have dramatic and emotional remembrances of being an Indian here in times long ago. Are the Anasazi coming back now to help in another Earth transition which may be in our near future? If so, are the Ant People preparing another evacuation of segments of another dying and/or doomed civilization?

▲ **Wall drawing left by the Anasazi. Note the similarity of these ancient figures to these current descriptions of modern alien encounters.**

Modern descriptions of alien encounters. ▶

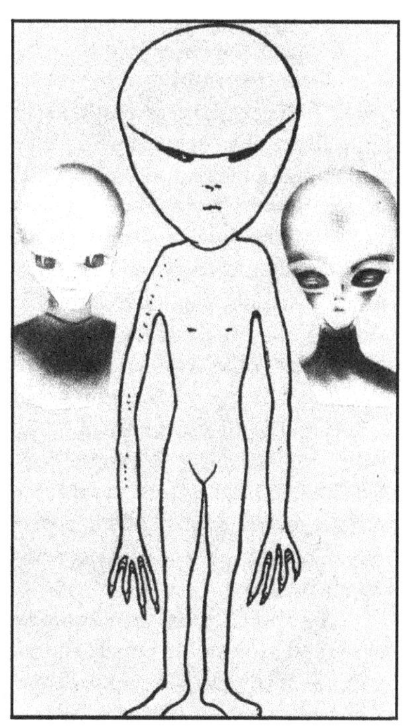

We may soon need to place ourselves in a frame of reference that will accommodate and accept direct answers to questions like these and many more that may be far more poignant and that pertain to us and our world. Few of these questions may, in the long run, be negative — but instead may be a great opportunity for those who can change and adapt.

UFOS, ETS, AND YOU
THE SAGA OF SECRET CANYON
June 1993

In the past four years, I have had indirect offers from two international magazines that specialize in paranormal and/or New Age subjects to do an article about Secret Canyon. I responded with a flat no.

I have avoided writing anything about Secret Canyon because I have felt that the subject was just too sensitive (and dangerous) in a number of ways. Whatever is, or was, in Secret Canyon has been very quiet for a year or more. Perhaps it has been closed down or deactivated.

Sedona has undergone a population and construction explosion in recent years, so it is possible that is the reason for the lack of or cessation of activity. Too much pressure, maybe.

I don't know the definite origin for the name Secret Canyon and I'm not sure if anyone else does, either.

Secret Mountain dominates the Secret Canyon area. Many of Sedona's major canyons basically terminate at or near Secret Mountain. They include Lincoln, Loy, Hartwell, Red, Fay, Boynton, Long, HS, Bear Sign and Secret Canyons. Secret Mountain is a sort of hub, like half a wagon wheel when viewed on a topographical map of these ten canyons.

Around 1920, several of the early ranchers of this area were riding horseback deep into Secret Canyon, probably looking for stray cattle. Some time during the day, the canyon became slowly filled by a dense bank of fog. Anyone who has lived around here for a long time and hikes the canyons will tell you that fog never occurs in the canyons. Once in a while, after a heavy rain or snow storm, thin fog will waft through a canyon, usually for only a few minutes. Evidently this particular fog was so thick the ranchers had to stop for the day and were a bit disoriented as to exactly where they were. Sudden dense fog materializing from nowhere is very typical of paranormal and UFO/alien activity.

During World War II, thousands of Chinese soldiers disappeared in China after a strange fog bank engulfed them. The same thing happened to a detachment of British soldiers in Europe storming a hill in 1944. Nothing of the British soldiers was ever found. In the China incident, all of the war equipment was strewn around but the soldiers were gone. This is not a rumor; it happened, and it has been written about in a number of books. It's well documented.

The two ranchers, while inside this fog, began to hear a great roaring sound which they thought was a freight train. They thought that somehow they had become lost and were near the Santa Fe Railroad tracks west of Flagstaff. Then an incredibly bright ball of light came off the rim of the canyon and descended down into the canyon. I don't know if anything happened right after that because that is all of the story I have. The next morning the fog cleared and the ranchers found that they were indeed still in Secret Canyon. That is the earliest unusual activity that I know of having occurred in Secret Canyon.

So it has been going on for some time. It did not begin with the advent of New Agers. Since 1920, many people have had very strange experiences in Secret Canyon. I've been asked innumerable times what I think it is that exists or existed in Secret Canyon or on Secret Mountain. My guess is that it is, or was, either a portal of some type or an entrance to an underground base or tunnel system of some sort. UFO activity here has always been clustered in the general vicinity of Secret Mountain/Secret Canyon. In fact, because I keep an unscientific account of this, I would say that 80 percent of all UFO activity in Arizona occurs near or in Secret Canyon or around Secret Mountain. The portal, or whatever, is/was centered about two-thirds of the way into Secret Canyon, a distance of about three miles from the mouth of the canyon.

Secret Canyon is about seven miles long in its entirety. The center of the activity may actually be on the side of Secret Mountain near Secret Canyon. Both areas are in quite remote locations. Some of the incidents that have occurred in Secret Canyon follow:

A number of hikers deep in Secret Canyon have been gripped suddenly by an overpowering fear and have literally run all the way out of the canyon. This includes a battle-hardened British Royal Marine who, before that, had not believed anything he had heard about Secret Canyon. This activity is entirely suggestive of some sort of device that is switched on. Sub-sonic sound waves perhaps, or some type of ELF (extra low frequency) device may account for this. People have had machine guns stuck in their noses in Secret Canyon (and in two other canyons) and have been told to turn back by men in black uniforms and, in two cases, by men wearing orange jumpsuits with a large insignia on either the right or left chest area. Very sloppy work by someone.

Sounds like hikers with great imaginations just getting a bit carried away? Not quite, and here's why. I have a friend who is retired from Army Intelligence and he has told me that, in fact, elite army units or teams, have been (or were at one time) very active in the Secret Canyon/Secret Mountain area. I inquired of him if he thought aliens might be involved in this mysterious activity, in conjunction with the U.S. Military. He answered in the affirmative. There is more to this but I am not going to go into it here.

As a point of interest, Navajo Army Depot, a munitions storage area now generally deactivated, lies only a few air miles north of Secret Mountain. The depot is about six miles long by five miles wide. A local wilderness guide was deep in Secret Canyon several years ago when he was knocked off his feet by something invisible (like a ray) and crawled on his hands and knees a quarter of a mile before he could get back on his feet. Unearthly buzzing sounds have been experienced by many hikers and campers who have said that these sounds have originated from deep in the ground. I've experienced this phenomenon myself and it is a very weird sound. Jet engine-like sounds going on and off have been heard in the area. At least a half dozen times UFOs have been seen slowly flying above Secret Canyon, shooting blazing beams of light into the canyon as if they were probing for something. Some of the witnesses to this were camped in Secret Canyon and the UFOs flew right over them. I wrote at length about these incidents in both The Alien Tide and in my new book, The Quest. Whenever I talk on this subject, I always point out that 99.9% of the hikers and campers who have ventured into Secret Canyon or onto Secret Mountain have had nothing adverse whatsoever happen to them. They enjoyed perfectly normal hiking or camping trips; so there is no real reason to avoid this area if you are inclined to go there. However, you will never find me camping in Secret Canyon — not in the back half anyway. So that's about it for Secret Canyon. There is a lot more but it's too wild and unverifiable to repeat here. I just hope that paranoia buffs don't get carried away with this.

Soldier's Pass Incident

I experienced an incident recently, probably not connected to Secret Canyon (but it could be), that I will briefly mention here, in closing. Several months ago I found a piece of aircraft fuselage about four feet long and two feet wide and painted a lime green color. This was in the area of Soldier's Pass. Several days after I found it, I took it up to the Sedona Airport terminal and just happened to run into an FAA official, a pilot and an aircraft mechanic, who were standing in the lobby. I was impressed. After examining it, the FAA official said that it probably was from a twin-engine Cessna that had crashed on Wilson Mountain in 1980. But, coincidentally, a friend of mine and a friend of his, a number of years ago near Loy Canyon, found small wreckage pieces of what an aircraft mechanic said was part of a Korean War-era jet fighter. It had evidently hit the ground a high rate of speed. I asked him if the pieces had any paint on them. He replied that some pieces had lime green paint on them. There have never been any reports, newspaper or otherwise, of a jet or jet fighter crashing in this area.

January 1995

In the last several months I've had a number of UFO-related incidents and experiences that have radically altered the way I look at the whole subject of flying aerial objects. I have personally come to the conclusion that many unidentified flying objects are in fact living singular entities that are interdimensional or can at least maintain a frequency that generally makes them invisible to the naked human eye. An added factor is that UFOs normally unseen often show up stunningly well with night-vision equipment or conventional binoculars but yet are invisible to the naked eye.

An example of this is the following incident. In this case conventional binoculars were used. On the night of September 15, 1994, a lot of UFO activity was seen in the Sedona area. Our UFO research group got together and decided to spread out over a wide area to get better coverage. There were six of us in four vehicles. We now have a CB radio network in this area. We can blanket an area of about a hundred square miles. I highly recommend a CB network for other UFO research groups who are having difficulty in maintaining a mobile communications system. Hand-held radios also work very well in conjunction with automobile CBs and/or base stations installed permanently in outlying homes. When an unusual object is spotted by one observer the others can quickly look in a specific direction or move to a better vantage point to record the activity, whatever it might be.

On the night of September 15 we stationed ourselves in diverse locations. Rob Meyers and I went to the west, to the canyonlands area of the Coconino National Forest. I was in position on Dry Creek Road and Rob was en route to the Loy Butte area about six miles farther to the west. The others were at Airport Mesa and Soldiers Pass. While waiting for Rob to reach his destination, I scanned the desert and buttes to the south with my binoculars. Almost immediately I spotted a very unusual flashing white light about two miles to the southwest. The light looked very much like a strobe, but it appeared to be a light by itself; it did not act in a manner that made it look like it was attached to a plane or a helicopter. The flashing light was at first about a thousand feel above the desert floor. With the naked eye this bright object was totally invisible. The light then moved downward and floated in an erratic pattern just above the desert floor. It rose up again to about a thousand feet and in seconds began a gradual vertical descent. The flashing light continued downward until it settled into an area of thick piñon pines.

I could not see the light itself at that point, but its flashes lit up a wide area in the pine forest. Then the light went out. Just before the light had descended into the trees, an object moved into position about four thousand feet above the flashing light. The object was a number of white and red lights in a triangular pattern, with one pulsing white light in its center. It remained in that position for about five minutes. It was not an aircraft, at least not a conventional aircraft. The hovering object was obviously either monitoring or accompanying the object/light that had settled into the trees.

The hovering object suddenly left and flew at a steady speed to the north about the same time Rob reached a good vantage point at Boynton Pass. The strobing object (now switched off) must have been still on the ground and Rob was coming near to its location but he could not see it.

Rob continued on to the Loy Butte area and pulled off on a high ridge where he had a panoramic view. At about that time I spotted through my binoculars two blood-red, pulsing balls of light at about 8000 feet descending at a 60-degree angle from the north. I could see them only with the binoculars even though they were no more than two miles way. Awesome is the only word to describe the sight of those deep-crimson-red pulsing lights. All of these objects that night moved in a manner that entirely suggested that they were living entities. In no way did they seem to be technical or mechanical in nature. I can say with complete confidence that when one witnesses something like this, life is never quite the same from that moment on. I've now seen over ten of these strange lights between May and October 1994. I've photographed four of them at close range.

On the CB I was almost beside myself with excitement, hoping Rob could get some good photos of the red balls, as he was much closer to the lights than I was. Unfortunately, Bear Mountain partially blocked a good view he might have had of the lights, but he still should have been able to see them. The two lights, independently pulsing that fuzzy red color, continued to descend at a 60-degree angle and I could see then that the red lights would end up in the same area that the strobe-like white lights had landed. The red lights continued their sliding descent, coming down behind a small hill about 200 yards to the west of where the white strobing object was last seen. The red lights also disappeared on the ground. We waited about an hour for the red or white lights to reappear, but they did not. Rob never saw the red pulsing lights. No one had any missing time or was bothered in any way.

In reference to the night-vision binoculars (as reported in last month's article), five of our group watched a white pulsing object about thirty feet in diameter rise from the base of Secret mountain and hover several thousand feet over the mountain as if studying us as we studied it. This object was totally invisible to the naked eye or through conventional binoculars. This is something I've never heard of before happening anywhere in the world. But it has recently happened a lot in this area, and multiple adult witnesses have been involved.

There has been a great deal of this type of activity in Midway, New Mexico (ten miles east of Roswell), in the last six months or so. Over 700 hours of video film of these highly unusual flying objects have been shot by a Midway resident. Most of the Midway film was shot in clear daylight, and the footage is extraordinary. No one has any idea what the flying objects are on the film, but they move much like living, flying entities.

PART 3

A PHOTO GALLERY OF THE SPIRIT OF SEDONA

Nothing is so contagious as example; and we never do any great good or evil which does not produce its like.

— La Rochefoucauld

From a little spark may burst a mighty flame.

— Dante

All I have seen teaches me to trust the Creator for all I have not seen.

— Emerson

Attempt the end, and never stand to doubt;
Nothing's so hard but search will find it out.

— Lovelace

When we do the best we can, we never know what miracle is wrought in our life, or in the life of another.

— **Helen Keller**

*Man's aim in life is not to add from day to day his material prospects
and to his material possessions, but his predominant calling
is from day to day to come nearer his Maker.*
— **Mahatma Gandhi**

Nature cannot be surprised in undress. Beauty breaks in everywhere.
— **Emerson**

Good is the only investment that never fails.

— Thoreau

Nothing with God can be accidental.

— **Longfellow**

That man is the richest whose pleasures are the cheapest.

— Thoreau

Whatever you can do, or dream you can, begin it.
Boldness has genius, power and magic in it.

— *Goethe*

Beauty is life when life unveils Her Holy Face.
But you are Life and you are the veil.
Beauty is eternity gazing at itself in a mirror.
But you are eternity and you are the mirror.

— **Khalil Gibran**

If you have knowledge, let others light their candles at it.
— **Margaret Fuller**

Like the sun, love radiates and warms into life all that it touches.
— **O.S. Marden**

Our thoughts are the epochs in our lives;
all else is but a journal of the winds that blew while we were here.
— **Thoreau**

Something great and wonderful is happening today, and I am part of it.
— Robert Scott

Write it in your heart that every day is the best day of your year.
— Emerson

I am not afraid of tomorrow, for I have seen yesterday, and I love today.
— **William White**

He is strong who conquers others: He who conquers himself is mighty.
— **Lao-Tse**

You are today where your thoughts have brought you;
you will be tomorrow where your thoughts take you.

— **James Allen**

What we obtain too cheap we esteem too little;
it is dearness only that gives everything its value.

— **Thomas Paine**

If you want your neighbor to know what the Christ Spirit will do your him, let him see what it has done for you.

— **Beecher**

I love to be alone. I never found the companion that was so companionable as solitude.

— **Thoreau**

Never forget that those who bring happiness to the lives of others cannot keep it from themselves.

— **Maurice Maeterlinck**

An honest heart possesses a kingdom.

— **Seneca**

Love is the light and sunshine of life. We are so constituted that we cannot fully enjoy ourselves, or anything else, unless someone we love enjoys it with us. Even if we are alone, we store up our enjoyment in hope of sharing it hereafter with those we love.

— **John Lubbock**

Nature is the living, visible garment of God.

— *Goethe*

I count him braver who overcomes his desires than him who conquers his enemies; for the hardest victory is the victory over self.

*— **Aristotle***

What is lovely never dies, but passes into other loveliness, star-dust, or seafoam, flower or winged air.

*— **Aldrich***

By the work one knows the workman.

— LaFontaine

Where there is peace, God is.

— Herbert

He who cherishes a beautiful vision, a lofty ideal in his heart, will one day realize it. Dream lofty dreams, and as you dream, so shall you become.
— **James Allen**

God has delivered yourself to your care,
and says, "I had no fitter to trust than you."

— ***Epictetus***

PART 4

REMOTE VIEWING

How to Talk to Spirits

I do indeed think that some type of protection is in order and certainly wise when one attempts to link up with the unseen and go beyond into the unknown. Again, protection can be worked in a number of forms. Asking a high spiritual being to watch over one, placing white light in and around the body, and using solid, clear-cut affirmations of protection are fine.

I would include here a caution about affirmations. People tend to be a bit wishy-washy about their convictions in an affirmation — in other words, vague, ineffective and doubting. Just saying the words won't do the job. One needs to be definite, decisive and forceful when using affirmations.

I was once given an affirmation and visualization technique I would like to share here with everyone. This was given to me by a woman who is a psychic healer. She travels the world alone and has had amazing "protection" down through the years. I have, over time, tried hundreds of affirmations and this is the only one I use with regularity. It seems to work well for me. Others may have a better one. It is as follows:

"I am filled and surrounded with the blazing white light of the beloved Creator. Nothing but good shall come to me. Nothing but good shall go from me. I give thanks. I give thanks. I give thanks. So be it."

Another method that works well for me is to fill my body with white light expanding to several feet out and then visualizing a layer of sparkling gold energy covering the white.

I also frequently use the Tibetan Ascended Master, Djwhal Khul's Ring Pass Not visualization of protection. I simply see a bright ring of white light around myself, three or four feet out, and affirm that any entity who would do me harm in any way cannot pass into the center of this ring.

These do seem to work very well for me. They are just several suggestions. There are many, many good ones in many, many books.

So now we are ready to begin to talk to spirits. To go into this with a lot of curiosity and a complete lack of fear and paranoia will help the process immeasurably. As we all know, fear on its own will generate many events and situations. We can create monsters that are entirely real to the mind but that in actuality do not exist at all. Higher beings on the other side are, for the most part more than willing to converse with us, especially once we get good at it. In a way it's like learning a foreign language. Eyes can be open or closed when doing this procedure. Sometimes it takes a great deal of concentration and in those instances I always keep my eyes closed. Sometimes the connection is so easy I can sit with my eyes open and talk freely and effortlessly with the unseen entity. That is when the experience is especially fun and educational.

When I communicate with unseen beings I usually wait until one happens by, like a pedestrian walking along, or until one is drawn by the "signal" I put out, a signal that I want to speak with an advanced being from Over There. For some reason I have never stayed very long with the same personality or entity. I prefer variety. Although, if I try hard enough, I can usually "call" a being whom I have talked to before. This is usually at the insistence of someone here, human on the Earth plane, who wants to talk to that particular being Over There. (Don't get me wrong, I don't do this all day every day. Two or three times a month is typical.) Sometimes I get a name from a being I am talking to and sometimes not. I have discovered that some of them are not in the least interested in names (labels). I think most, if not all, of them do have a name of sorts. But I get the impression that most of them Over There in the invisible realms recognize each other by individual vibration. When they want to talk to someone else Over There somewhere, what they do is feel and think and visualize that other being's vibration. The called being feels and sees that call and comes to the summons if it can.

I'm not sure how much actual distance there is between those of the unseen worlds and us, at least distance in the way we might think of it, like forty million miles or something. The distance, in reality, may be vast or it may not exist at all. It is better not to think in terms of distance, putting it out of mind. If we think in terms of distance it will hinder us. We first focus in our minds with certainty that we can have and will have a beneficial link with the Other Side. We know that we can easily bridge the gap that separates the worlds. If you don't believe you really can do all this, you never will. But when you know and believe with confidence and conviction that it really is as simple and as easy as picking up a phone and talking to someone, then it will work. Simple. Simplicity is always the key. Never assume anything when dealing with the other side, no preconceived notions or ideas, just let it happen. It will *always* be different from what one expects. We humans tend to intellectualize things to death. We should remember simplicity, and not strain. This process should be as easy as we can make it.

When I begin the initial contact with an unseen being I always see developing in my mind (it might turn out to be different for others) a rather foggy bluish-colored void. In a few minutes a being will usually approach and enter into this void. It's very important that my mind be relaxed, rather indifferent and in neutral. I don't strain. I can't have ten competing thoughts jamming and confusing the process, such as what I am going to have for supper, the repair bill or some other distraction. I "feel" the being coming. They, Over There, radiate a vast variety of energies. This is easy now that I have become sensitive to it. Some of these beings, I have found, are more powerful, more wise and more knowledgeable than anything I can put into words. Some of them are just sheer, awesome power.

I see them in my mind usually in one of three ways. One, a luminescent, human-like form; two, a ball of light; or three, a clearly defined and detailed entirely physical looking human form. They may take the human form to make it easier to relate to them, or it may be that they were recently human somewhere and still retain that form. The ones that are orbs of light are *always* the great and powerful ones. The lightbeings (orbs) are the powerful ones and the lights can be any color or combination of colors. The colors are always incredibly beautiful and have a silvery radiance to them.

Now, once I feel or see a being nearby who is willing to converse, it is important that I avoid thoughts of being lowly, insignificant or unworthy. If I see myself as I did in the early going as a mere meek, insignificant human, hoping, on my knees, to talk to some lofty and regal superior being, chances are they won't even bother to make the effort to connect — at least not for long, anyway. We shouldn't worship them, prostrate ourselves before them or be supplicating to them, but polite and respectful — yes. If we will honestly make a determined effort to mentally talk with one of these beings as an equal, as a serious student, we will get rewarding and satisfying results. Sometimes they have to be extremely patient while we grope with the process but if they see that we are really in earnest and sincere they will in most cases try hard to accommodate us. If we *believe* that it is possible to speak to them, *it will be.*

I have found, and I have done this quite often, that what greatly aids this process is having a close friend present who will ask specific questions through me and then wait for the answer from the spirit being. The back-and-forth process will be clearer and easier. I have never had an experience with this with what might be termed a negative entity. But if the contact feels bad in any way, break off contact at once, drop it for that day and then try it again at a later date. Having other live people in the room somehow makes the signal clearer and stronger.

This is in a way like channeling, but the big difference is that one doesn't go into any kind of trance or altered state. Another definite advantage of this direct contact method over channeling is that I can mull over and think about the being's answer before I relay it to the listener. Sometimes after hearing the answer I may not *want* to relay it to the questioner at all. I have been in this situation a number of times and often the spirit being will leave it entirely up to me. I might choose to rephrase the answer so it will be more palatable to the one who asked. Spirit beings I have discovered can be very, very blunt. I mean no sugar coating, point blank, black and white, blunt.

Something that I do once in a while, although I don't print up flyers for this, is contact a "dead" relative to get vital information for a friend, or relative still here on the Earth plane. All I usually need is the full name of the dead person. It's really an incredible affirmation and reward when I get vital personal information that only the dead person could have known. I have now done this on many occasions.

The beings Over There, almost all of them, rarely communicate with each other in words. Over There they have a universal language that is instantly conveyed in feelings and pictures. They will rarely speak to us or to their own friends and associates in words. We have to get used to this. Also keep in mind that beings Over There don't sit around all day and night waiting for us to try to engage them in conversation. It's really quite low on their priority list, I think. Many of them, if not most, have a lot of things to do and may be taking time out of what may be an important and busy schedule to patiently try to talk with us. This is something that always bothers me about channeling. It must be, at times, an enormous imposition on a higher being when a human channel that particular being is committed to just sits down and starts channeling with no prior request for time of the higher being or any mental notification by the channeler. We need to treat them with the same courtesy, respect and diplomacy we would give to a respected, cherished and honored friend. Some beings are always absolutely delighted and charmed to get a chance to interact with us, but then there will be a few who will be short and impatient with us. Just like Earth people, a personality is a personality, here or Over There in the invisible worlds. But to talk to and be in the direct light and presence of a Universal Entity who may be millions or billions of years ahead of you in evolution is a feeling of wonderment and awe that has to be experienced to be fully appreciated.

We all know the saying "one picture is worth a thousand words." It's true and that's basically how they communicate with each other in the invisible realms. We in turn have to translate those pictures and the feelings which go with them which they transmit to us. It's fun, especially once you get a rapid-fire, back-and-forth transaction going with a particular entity. (And the entity might never have been a human!) It takes a bit of trial and error for a while. The effort however, is always worth it. It is a real pleasure, when at times you get a being who is willing or able to talk to you freely in good clear English (or whatever your native language is). Maybe only one out of four entities will or can do this.

We tend to think of them as perfect and flawless. Some of them are close to that but from my experience I can tell you that most of them have a terrific sense of humor and many of them have a temper of sorts. They never fly off the handle and react to things the way we often do but they can get icy blunt and stern at times. I have on several occasions had them lose patience with me, cut the session off and leave at that point. Just like us, their patience does have its limits. I tell some dyed-in-the-wool spiritual people stuff like this and they are often aghast and insulted that an ascended master would have a spicy sense of humor or, God forbid, a *temper*! Believe it. Those of the higher realms are not that much different from us except that they have made all the mistakes we are making now. They have gone beyond these mistakes and they are not about to get too close to the earth cycle and get caught up in it again. I have seen that they do often differ and disagree with each other. It takes the form of a friendly and mature disagreement. At the higher levels they never have shoving and shouting arguments. I've listened during a heated back-and-forth conversation, among two or more of these high entities debating a question in point. Usually, after a few minutes of rather intense banter, higher beings will settle on a consensus or just drop the whole matter altogether with no hard feelings. They know when to quit. These beings, once one gets used to their demeanor and appearance, are absolutely marvelous to be around, and the contact is *always* a fabulous learning experience. Once, in a question-and-answer session I had with four or five people in Colorado, a man, through me, asked an impossible question of a spirit. I think it was something about a personal relationship. There was a long pause and then the entity replied to me with a hearty chuckle, "He has got to be joking!"

By now I'm sure some readers are wondering how I have come to have this incredible ability but I don't know absolutely everything about everything. Anyone who gets into this will discover that there are some things that they of higher levels flat will not let us see or give us specific, exact information about. I ask hard, tough questions. They will instead, often give a generality and then clam up entirely when pressed point blank on a specific question. I have at times had them say, "We (or I) will not answer that" or they simply don't answer at all. Silence. This really irritates some people who want to know everything past, present and future, right now. We are here to discover and to learn. If invisible entities told us everything we wanted to know, they would probably be defeating the very purpose of why we, as humans, are alive here on the Earth. I firmly believe now that all of them who have earned great knowledge and wisdom are bound by some sort of law or regulation that they cannot (at this time) under any circumstance divulge certain information to us. We must find out these answers on our own. "Seek and ye shall find." They, Over There, cannot violate, under severe penalty, these nondisclosure-to-Earth-humans rules. That's how it works. This is not a free ride and we have to work hard to get out of here and to earn the right or privilege to be where the great spiritual ex-humans go. They earned the privilege and now, in turn, so do we. Yogananda, Yukteswar, Djwhal Khul, Babaji, Dadaji, Lahiri Mahasaya and Kuthumi are some of those who were human like we are and gained the knowledge and wisdom and love to leave here and to go to a higher, grander place.

There is I think, but I am not positive, some kind of a simple "secret." It's the ticket out of here. I'm not precisely sure what "it" is but I have been ever so close to discovering it on several occasions. All of the Great Masters who are now no longer physically among us had discovered or were told that secret. I think more of us long ago would have discovered the Secret except that we come from either such a deep profit framework or a deep intellectual motivational framework that we simply cannot see the Secret. The Great Secret. Simple. Look closely at the photographs of the few great masters who have allowed their pictures to be taken. Look at their facial expressions. I think it is pretty evident that they know what the secret is and are leaving the rest for us students to discover for ourselves. Yes, indeed, love is part of the secret, but love is only a vital component of it. There's more.

When I, hopefully, earn or gain the right to learn "it", I am out of here.

I'm just being practical. (I am not one who believes all is perfect no matter what form it takes. That may work for some but not for myself. I need to categorize.) I know this ain't where it's at. I've seen what it's like Over There and personally that's where I want to be and to stay.

So, talking with beings on the other side is not particularly difficult but one has to work at it. Practice it. Good luck.

How to Learn Remote Viewing

I have in the past refrained from teaching remote viewing, even though I've often been asked to, because I know what a few people would do with it. They would use it for the advancement of themselves at the expense of another. In other words they would spy on someone. I am going to explain how to do remote viewing here and I am going to ask that, once learned, this ability never be used to hurt or take advantage of another person or sensitive creature in any way, shape, form or manner. I won't go into it in depth in this book, giving examples, but if we use a God-given gift or privilege like remote viewing for greed, revenge or any form of destructive negativity we will in time pay a dear and great price for it. It's the Universal Law. The way it is.

So that it is clear that I am not blowing smoke about remote viewing and how it works (and that I know how it works), I'll give readers the opportunity to validate the existence of it for themselves. It's been satisfactorily proven by Russian and American researchers that remote viewing is not a psychic ability. It is a psychometric ability that can be taught to anyone, at least anyone who has a serious desire to learn the technique and commit to it a measure of dedicated effort. I learned remote viewing more or less by accident. In the remote viewing business I am known as a "natural". These following examples indicate my use and knowledge of remote viewing.

In the winter of 1991 I had gone to meet Tom O'Donnell, a psychologist friend, who was staying at a local motel. We were going to go to lunch. But I had to wait for Tom as he was still typing up a patient's report on his lap-top computer. While waiting, I sat on a bed and started browsing through a travel magazine. My mind quickly began to wander, as it often does, and I found myself daydreaming about nothing in particular. Tom owned a home near Durango, Colorado. The house sat on a high mesa and had a splendid, sunny, dining room that looked out onto the Animas River Valley. All of a sudden, to my surprise, I found my daydream centered on that dining room, and the vision of the dining room was so clear and vivid it seemed as though I were actually there. I found that I was looking down at Tom's large oak dinner table. The sun was shining on it brightly. Along with that I had strong visual impressions of the entire contents of the room and the rooms adjoining it. The early afternoon sun flooding through the windows gave the scene a rather smoky, eerie and alive feeling.

During this lucid vision of the dining room something drew my attention to what was lying on the far right corner of the dining room table. "Looking" closer I saw that it was my first two books, *The Mysteries of Sedona* and *The Alien Tide*. Looking still closer I saw that one book was on top of the other and they were both face down. The visual impression of all this was so clear and brilliant it disturbed me. I had never before experienced anything like this. This was just not normal. There was something entirely different about this daydream. I thought about the vision for a minute and then interrupted Tom as he worked at his computer. I said, with a great degree of hesitation and reservation, "Tom. At home, did you leave two of my books on the right corner of your dining room table, face down?"

He stopped typing, thought about it, then replied, "Why yes, I believe I did. I don't know if they were face down but I think I did leave them on the table." Then he asked why I had asked.

I answered that it was odd but I thought I could actually see the books there. He was intrigued by what I said and asked if there was anything else I could see. (As a psychologist he knew about remote viewing; at the time I had never even heard of the term.) While "standing" there in the far-away dining room and "looking" (I could do this in the motel room with my physical eyes either open or closed), I swung my rather foggy, dreamlike gaze and discovered I could not only see everything in the far-away room but could "float" around in any direction or any angle I desired to get a better or closer look at anything in the house. It was a wonderful and new experience but quite frightening at the same time. I, or at least part of me, was actually and literally in that dining room 350 miles away in Colorado. Yet I was, at the same time, sitting in the motel room in Cottonwood, Arizona. The part of me that was there in Durango gazing about in that far-away room could see with complete but dreamlike full-color clarity every single item within range of what would be normal sight.

Tom had at the time recently completed a glass-enclosed greenhouse, part of which now abutted the dining room. You had to look through the dining room and greenhouse windows to see the mountain and valley panorama outside. As a final touch he had stocked the greenhouse with tropical plants, birds and fish. I floated, with no effort except the desire to do so, through the dining room, through the living room and with no resistance through a closed glass door into the new greenhouse. I had never seen the greenhouse and had no prior exact knowledge of its contents. While floating (it felt absolutely comfortable and weightless) through the greenhouse I described the species and colors of every single one of the half dozen or so birds that were flying free in the temperature controlled greenhouse. I described the number and sizes of the Oriental goldfish in a small corner pool. Many of the tropical plants were in bloom and although I had no idea what the plants were, with 100% accuracy I described the colors, shapes and sizes of the flowers. If I wanted a closer look I found that effortlessly I could glide to within inches of whatever I wanted to look at.

The birds in the greenhouse got very spooked and nervous when I did this to them. I tried this experiment several times months later with Tom's small dog, Binky. Binky would stare straight back at me, acting like the whole thing was perfectly normal. Tom and I were *both* amazed at what happened that day at the motel. We agreed to do some in-depth experimenting with this odd discovery at a later date.

In the ensuing weeks I found that I could "go" to Tom's house with ease at any time of the day or night. On "arrival" I always found myself outside the house, high over a point above his driveway and looking down at his two-story home. I would then drift around until I located Tom. With a bit of concentrated effort I could almost always get his attention. This was getting to be great fun for both of us — especially me. When I "dropped in," usually in midafternoon, Tom was usually either out working in his garden, doing something in the kitchen or working at his computer. Unless he was completely preoccupied I could often telepathically let him know I was going to call him on the phone soon. (Sometimes he was where he couldn't hear the phone ring.) I would do this by bugging him to get his attention. I would telepathically shout something like, "Hey Tom, it's Tom. I'm going to call you at 3:30," or something like that. After a while he could recognize when I was around. Often he would stop what he was doing and go to the phone just as it rang.

I've tried this with other people with mixed results, but Tom and I got very good at it. I was always careful not to drop in at odd or unscheduled times so as not to intrude on Tom's privacy, which I did do on several early occasions when I was trying out this new-found phenomenon. What I was doing with these experiments was additionally interesting for me because I think it is almost exactly what spirits deal with when they want to get our attention or talk to us. During these visits I was a "spirit" myself.

Tom and I decided to do a sort-of-scientific, sort-of-clinical test of my developing remote-viewing abilities. We selected a day a week in advance. He was to collect a variety of different items and objects selected by him and which were completely unknown to me. He was to arrange this stuff in his living room. At the appointed time I was to travel there and try to remote view the objects he had readied for me. The day came. It was a Thursday. The agreed-upon time was 4:30 in the afternoon. Always one to do things a little differently, I decided I would "go" up to Durango a half hour early and eavesdrop. I thought I might get a preview of the odds and ends he had arranged for me in the living room. Tom is a bit of a nonconformist himself so I figured I'd stay a step ahead of him.

I arrived as usual over the spot above the driveway, drifted downward and glided effortlessly through the wall of Tom's second story office. (If you think this sounds crazy, wait until you try it!) I went through his office and glided down and around the spiral staircase. As I got near the kitchen, which is on the ground level, suddenly and instantly I was seized by a feeling of absolute, utter panic. Some sort of unnameable psychic alarm was going off inside me. I had a feeling of terror. I felt as if I were going to be ambushed in some way. I stopped at once and looked around. I took my time, but everything seemed all right. I quickly brushed the feeling off. Simple paranoia. There was no reason for so much alarm. I continued on. Tom was in the kitchen dressed in a red plaid shirt, blue jeans and cowboy boots. He didn't know I was there. He was cooking something that smelled spicy and sweet. That has been the only time so far that I have psychically smelled anything. The feeling of alarm, although lessened, was still with me. It worried me and annoyed me. The feeling would not go away.

Could it be, I thought, that some unseen, unknown agency, perhaps even alien, that I could not see or sense was preparing to attack me here and now? After all, I was a complete and total rank novice at this. The nagging feeling of an ambush again was bothering me greatly. I picked up the phone and called Tom. I told him that I had already been there, I told him what he was wearing and asked him what it was that he was cooking. With some amusement and amazement he replied that it was barbecue sauce and he confirmed that he was wearing exactly what I had just described. Before I got to the ambush thing he mentioned that his dog Binky had run off earlier in the day and he was concerned about the dog's whereabouts. I paused for a second and then told him the dog was at the front door. I could see the dog through the walls. He put the phone down. I heard the front door open, then a laugh and a bark. Binky loved to take off. I could always locate Binky in a second. He didn't stand a chance when I was around.

Tom was supposed to be alone in the house at 4:30 on that Thursday afternoon. I said, "Tom, is someone in the living room ... sitting on the couch?" Sheepishly, he admitted that there was. He had asked, unbeknownst to me, a neighbor to come over and be a witness to the experiment. This was perfectly okay with me, and that evidently had been the reason for the ambush sensation. For some reason I could not see the neighbor at all but I could by then sense him. A little later, even with strained effort, I got the neighbor's physical appearance and clothing entirely wrong. I wasn't even close. *I could not see the man.* (Since then there has been some interesting conjecture on this occurrence.) It was then that I discovered that there were and are some things I can not see no matter how hard I try.

We then began the prearranged test. Tom had placed the eight or ten small objects on his living room coffee table. I could quite plainly see a tall green plant on the table and I said (we were still on the phone)that I could not see the other objects. The plant was too big. First hit! The last time I had been to his house he had not had a plant on or near the coffee table. Tom took the plant, a cactus, off the coffee table and placed it on the floor.

I soon discovered another peculiarity. I could only see objects that were in direct sunlight! (This is not always the case.) The objects he held up out of the direct sunlight were in shadows so dark to my vision that I could not make them out at all. Ultimately, I got about 50% of the objects correct. My best hit was when he held up a large, framed photo. This was a tough one but with concentrated effort I said that it was a face and it took up a large area of the picture. I said it was in a shiny copper frame and there was a tree in the photo to the right of the face. Tom returned with, "Well, you are basically right about the face and frame but there is no tree in the photo." Then a few moments later he realized there was an added factor. He said that a reflection of his ten-foot tall ficus tree was on the glass to the right of the face and that was the tree that I had seen. I was looking over his right shoulder as he moved the framed photo around in the sunlight so I could see it better. I kept saying things like, "a little to the right, to the left, up, down, now tip it forward" and so forth. I could see all of this clearly while he held the phone to his ear.

I could go on with many verified examples like this but I think you get the idea. Here, then, is how to learn to do remote viewing. It is very simple. It just takes the effort. If nothing verifiable happens at first, don't worry about it. Keep trying. In the beginning do not try this or talk about this with anyone who is going to ridicule you or make fun of you over it. That will kill it dead if you are a beginner because it will anchor in you a belief that remote viewing is not real and you can't do it. Self-confidence is shaky enough in matters like this. That is, without doubt, the biggest obstacle I had to overcome in remote viewing and especially in the early stages of psychic experimentation and communication with the other side. I had to believe that I could do it. A willingness to accept mistakes and failures and to keep trying are definite attributes. A thick skin sometimes helps, too. There is only one other non-military source that I know of that teaches remote viewing and the lengthy course that they offer is expensive.

Let's start gradually with a beginning exercise. If you know someone who lives a hundred miles or so away from you who is a person you respect and trust like mom or dad or a brother, sister, or close friend and who lives in an area or a house you love to go to, it will make it much easier for you. Deep familiarity with a place facilitates the process. Preferably, you should choose a place in a lovely and quiet country setting. It certainly could be a city setting too, if it's quiet. But a big city makes it more difficult because of all the distractions of traffic noises, horns blaring, sirens, aircraft, tires screeching, gunfire and so on. I need to emphasize that distance is not at all a limiting factor. If you live in California, for example, and your trusted friend lives in Georgia, that's fine, but a distance of 100 to 300 miles away seems to be a good practice distance at first. But don't be overly concerned about distance; don't let it restrict you. I have done remote viewing at a distance of over 6000 miles with verifiable accuracy.

Practice on your own, confidentially and by yourself at first. Choose a quiet, relaxed, unpressured time and in your mind, as in a daydream, go to the home of that trusted person, whom you have told what you are doing. It can be any location you choose but you must be *intimately familiar* with that location. At first it must be a place you have previously been to a number of times. Position yourself mentally on the front lawn where this person lives or on the porch, in a room, under a big shady tree or wherever it is comfortable and secure for you. Again, it has to be a spot you love and that you know intimately. Imagine yourself being there, for real, on that beautiful and enjoyable spot.

Now, while you are there at your chosen spot, "look" all around you just as if you are really there and you have eyes to see everything. What is the day like? Is it warm, cool, raining or foggy, windy or hot and humid, snowing or cloudy or sunny? Take careful note of all that you "see." Details. Is the grass a nice rich green. Is the sky blue or white overcast? Is there a gentle breeze stirring that makes leaves rustle and limbs sway back and forth? Is it beginning to rain? Snow? Whose car or cars are parked in the driveway? What colors are the cars? Are there kids playing in the pool, on the grass, or having a snowball fight? Are there flowers blooming in the garden? With your "vision" go and inspect things more closely. Move right up to them to get a better look. A clearer look. How many roses are blooming in the rose patch? Count them. Are they white, yellow, red or pink? Go up close and look. Forget that you are two hundred miles away and "be" there. Daydream yourself there vividly. Practice these examples. You may want to go to several different locations in one session — maybe your favorite place in the Great Smokies or the Rockies, perhaps a secluded cove on a lake — it can be anywhere that you have a fondness in your heart. Do these practice runs for a few weeks or until you feel you are ready to go on to the next step.

The next step would be to include the person whose house you have been "visiting." This person has to be willing to participate in your learning experience. Do all of this with an almost childlike attitude of fun and adventure with no pressure. While the person is on the phone (be sure not to call when he or she is getting ready to go to work or to bed, or is busy making dinner) ask him, after you have "looked," if the day is, for example, sunny but very windy. Does it look like it rained hard earlier because there seem to be several large puddles of water in the yard? Is there a pile of loam or fertilizer on the front lawn because you see something dark brown and mound-shaped? That looks like a big stack of new lumber near the shed; is someone building something near the garden? Is that a new yellow tablecloth on the dining room table? You will probably find at first that you get almost everything wrong except for one or two direct or indirect hits. Those one or two hits will make you a firm believer and you will want more, much more.

Meditation, Remote Viewing, Spontaneous Viewing, and "Barriers"

When I was initially experimenting with remote viewing, one day a friend, while we were on the phone, asked if I could see anything unusual near the front of the house. I was highly intrigued by the challenge and it was a fun and harmless test. I "looked" and "floated" around outside and replied that I thought I could see a large black and red mechanical object on the lawn. I hesitated with caution and ventured that I thought that it looked like a larger than usual garden rototiller. The exciting and gratifying answer was that it was indeed a large red and black garden rototiller. Direct hit! So that's it. That is how easy it is. You can use this ability to explore the world — free. I have. You can go to other planets, stars, galaxies and dimensions. You can visit alien civilizations or take a careful look at UFOs.

You can do just about anything as long as it is not harmful to anyone or anything, but be intelligent about it; this ability is not a toy. You will find that other-worldly entities will often detect you as soon as you arrive. Either you will be allowed and welcomed to stay or you will be warned away. The warnings are clear-cut and decisive. You will get the message loud and clear so heed those warnings. Don't hang around to see if they are bluffing, because they are not.

You will also discover that you will encounter areas that are off limits to psychic travelers and have barriers. These barriers are like glass shields or glass walls and *usually* cannot be penetrated. I won't go into these barriers in this book but I will say that they have been the subject of intensely serious research and probing by Russian and American scientists and certain American military intelligence units. I know the latter to be a fact because I heard it from a U.S. Army General during a lecture. The only reason he commented on it was that someone pressed him hard on the question. He was very reluctant to talk on that particular subject.

There aren't many drawbacks to remote viewing, but there are a few. Spontaneous viewing is one of them. You will be going about mundane daily activities and you will sometimes without warning or trying see something in your mind that is transpiring somewhere else. In a romantic relationship I had several years ago my girlfriend was seeing someone else at the same time and didn't tell me. It had been going on for months. In my mind I watched her having hot, x-rated sex with a man — and it wasn't me. Not a great way to find out, but as it turned out the mental pictures were 100% accurate. A great plot for a soap opera.

Remember, too, that in remote viewing you will not see things as clearly as you do with your physical vision. You will have to learn to see in a different way because in remote viewing, places and things are ethereal, rather hazy and dreamlike, although at times the scene or location can be razor-sharp vivid. A lot of what you see and experience you will have no way to validate but it will always be a great, exciting, experimental adventure. Good luck.

I think that in many ways remote viewing is similar to out-of-body experiences or out-of-body travel. I am not, for some reason, much interested in OBEs but am very well-informed on the subject. I would rather go "traveling" by keeping my mind, body and self in one place and look around by extension. In remote viewing you have far more control. There is a distinct and definite similarity and yet a distinct and definite difference between remote viewing and an out-of-body experience. If you have a curiosity about out-of-body experiences or a need to know, read Robert Monroe's books *Journeys Out of Body* and *Far Journeys*. Read *Journeys Out of Body* first as the books are one and two in a series.

Some sort of a background in meditation is an enormous advantage in enabling us to view or visit normally unseen worlds. It brings us closer to God, too. Meditation is important because it trains one to quiet the mind. A quiet, still mind is essential for higher spiritual or psychic learning. We have to control the runaway, spontaneous babble which often, perhaps usually, rules the mind. It is painfully difficult for most of us to sit absolutely still for ten minutes without our minds taking off in a stream of thoughts that go in twenty different directions. Controlling, or getting control of, the mind, is difficult for many of us, especially these days with all the worries and situations that we have to deal with. Perhaps some can keep in check the runaway thoughts of the mind without a background in meditation. That's good. It means they have very good patterns of discipline and are well on their way to being in a position to see the unseen and watch the watchers who constantly watch us. This, I think, goes hand in hand with meditation and a calm and peaceful mind. It's a doubly interesting experience for the reason that once unseen entities know that we can indeed see them during meditation and have gone to the effort to learn to see them, there is a tremendous amount of respect for us on their part. They aren't used to humans looking back at them.

Although they somehow know that we are first-grade beginners no matter how good we get at it, they will very often coax and encourage us along patiently so that we can expand our experience into their worlds. Most of them are happy to, more than willing to share their existence with us. They can do the magnificent things they do and why shouldn't we be able to do the same? When we finally, as a race, break free of the self-imposed chains that hold us suspended in time and space we will, as a unit, join with them and they are glad for this also. I am sure. I am sure also that there have been nations or civilizations on Earth that have done just that in the distant past, civilizations and groups that have reached a state of perfection of spiritual and psychic consciousness, left their Earth bodies en masse and migrated to a better place somewhere Out There. These may include the residents of Anqkor Wat in Cambodia, Chaco Canyon (Anasazi) in New Mexico, Machu Picchu in Peru, and Tiahuanaco in Bolivia to mention just a few. It may well be that some of those same former Earth inhabitants are coming back to help us now. Hopefully, when they see that many of us are beginning to journey beyond the boundaries of the mundane, human, material world, they of the higher realms will stretch to give us all the assistance they can. But we have to move toward them; they *will not* do it for us. One step toward them, two steps towards us. I believe the Hundredth Monkey Principle will apply soon. It may be that one of us or someone else in some part of the world will be the hundredth monkey who sparks the spontaneous explosion that will free humanity from the bonds and chains of materialism and allow us to join the greater, liberated worlds of the unseen — in the unseen. This is all a part of meditation and meditation is part of the foundation that inspiration and innovation and creation spring from.

In meditation there are many methods and styles. For our purpose here I am not stressing reaching the Hindu samadhi euphoric levels of meditation. I don't think I have ever reached that state and it is, in my opinion, not essential for accessing the unseen worlds. Some spiritual or meditation books claim that samadhi is a necessary factor in reaching the higher worlds but I personally would find points of disagreement with that. My own meditation method utilizes the visualization of vibrant color. I don't meditate as often as I used to but in the beginning I had a meditation regimen which entailed sitting in a comfortable position for an hour or more every morning and visualizing filling my body, every cell, with vibrant, blazing, divine color. I did this for years. I use the colors red, blue, green, bluegreen, yellow, orange, violet, silver, white, pink and finally gold. It usually takes an hour to go from color to color. After a few months of this something in me began opening up and coming alive. That's the best way I (and others) can describe the experience. Sitting for a few minutes or an hour or more in the blackness of the mind either puts one to sleep or bores one so badly that one quickly loses interest in meditation. The mind needs something to work on, to concentrate on as we are meditating. For me it was working with colors. There are scores of excellent books on the market about meditation. In beginning meditation, we can choose a method that will work the best for us individually, a method that we are comfortable with. Again, we *have* to be able to go beyond the constant babble of the conscious mind in order to reach unseen worlds and unseen levels.

PART 5

INTERVIEWS

The following interviews are with Sedona residents who share their feelings, their knowledge, and their experiences.

Three questions were asked in the interviews:

- What drew you to Sedona?
- How has Sedona affected you?
- Why do you think Sedona is such a mysterious place?

Susan A. Stavoy
Psychic Reader

I lived in San Francisco, and after years of working in insurance, I resigned. Afterward I worked part-time in a gallery and did odd jobs — anything to stay out of big business.

In February of 1990 a friend asked me about Sedona, but I had never heard of it. After that, though, it seemed as if every other person I met had just been to Sedona or was going to be moving there. Finally, in April, 1990, I had decided to take my vacation several months later in June and spend a week in Sedona.

I was at the time studying rather intensively in San Francisco with a metaphysical teacher who had appeared in my life in February, when I had first heard of Sedona. We were meeting every week and I was continually challenged to expand my psychic and spiritual awareness — my consciousness of various levels of reality.

By May, my San Francisco studies had intensified to the point where I was receiving instruction during my meditations from my spiritual guides. Then I began to hear a voice in my head which said, "Move to Sedona." It kept repeating, "Move to Sedona. Move to Sedona." Over and over.

I *had* to pay attention to that voice. Without telling family or friends, or my teacher either, I quit my job, gave up the lease on my apartment and made arrangements to sell my furniture. I still had never been to Sedona, yet I *knew* I had to be there. When I allowed myself to examine everything I had been through over the past year I realized it had all been in preparation for moving to Sedona.

As if I had been under some kind of compulsion, I had quit my 9-to-5 job a year in advance. I needed to detoxify, to get that experience out of my system before I got to Sedona. Then hearing about Sedona and finding my teacher were the next steps. I know I was very fortunate to have had the months of spiritual preparation in San Francisco I received prior to moving here.

I did then take my vacation in Sedona and managed to check out the job market and find a place to stay. I went back to San Francisco, gathered up what few belongings I had left after my apartment sale, and moved to Sedona.

After I had lived in Sedona for three months, I had an out-of-body experience that changed my life. During a meditation with two friends I spontaneously left my body and traveled to meet energy beings who spoke with me about what would happen in my life.

I had done hand analysis [palmistry] in San Francisco for 15 years, in addition to my regular job, but after that out-of-body experience I found myself able to see and read auras much more clearly. I was inspired then — actually, compelled is a better word — to write a book about my experiences.

I completed that book in two months. While I was writing it, I was advised by my guides that it was actually the first book of a trilogy. They told me the names of the other books and what they would be about. So now I'm working on editing the first book while writing the second one.

Whether these things would have happened to me had I not moved to Sedona, I can't say, but I believe I came here so they could happen.

I've always referred to Sedona as Sedona University. I feel everyone who is *supposed* to be here, gets here, whether for a weekend seminar or a year-long post-doctoral independent study program. Sometimes people arrive to be teachers and sometimes students. The bottom line is, if Sedona wants you here you have no choice, no other option. Just like I did, you have to "Move to Sedona."

(*Author's note:* Susan had another interesting experience I would like to mention. While purchasing a newer vehicle for the move to Sedona, she was waiting in the salesman's office in San Francisco — mentally debating if the move to Sedona was the right thing to do. She glanced up and there on the office wall was a large framed color photo of Sedona's Cathedral Rock.)

Celeste
Visionary Artist

When I learned that Serapis Bey, the ascended master of the 4th ray of ascension, had moved his etheric center from Luxor, Egypt, to Sedona, Arizona, I wanted to come to Sedona. At the time, I was living in a Houston, Texas, suburb, and just beginning my spiritual commitment and developing my visionary art. Miraculously, the universe arranged for me to be in Sedona for the first time during the Harmonic Convergence in 1987. I had such a powerful experience that I announced to my husband (now ex-husband), "I'm going to live here someday!" It took four years and a total change in consciousness and lifestyle, but here I am.

I have meditated at all the vortexes many times, recording my experiences in paintings and drawings. First of all, I have made a deep connection with Master Serapis who originally drew me to Sedona. On Bell Rock I first saw the radiant entrance to his etheric city over Sedona. At Cathedral Rock I painted the double helix vortex beneath the crystal city. (See painting). Other visions — of the ascension chamber, of the open doorway between dimensions and of Master Serapis standing at the open gateway — have been recorded in paintings. Recently, I have received information for a course on ascension from Master Serapis which my husband, Jananda, and I are sharing as a four-week class.

At Airport Vortex, I had my first profound experience with Native American energy. My painting, "Sedona Ceremony," illustrates this event. As I was meditating, I found myself in a ceremony to build up courage for

Sedona Ceremony, by Celeste

the coming battle. An orange robe was placed over my shoulders. White Eagle and my spirit guide, White Cloud, each gave me white feathers. I felt their support and encouragement for the work ahead. The next day, during a hike to Boynton Canyon, I found two white feathers tied to a branch and dancing in a ray of sunlight deep in the forest. I knew they were a gift from Spirit confirming my connection with this sacred land.

In Boynton Canyon I have had many past-life experiences. I was shown my visits to this area as an etheric space being. I would come and go on space ships, helping the native people to establish a refuge for the survivors of the sinking Lemuria.

In general, Sedona has been a powerful influence on my personal ascension, helping me to assimilate past lives, present purposes and future self into my consciousness. My paintings reflect this profound expansion.

I think Sedona is the focus for the ascension flame of Master Serapis Bey for the planet. Of course there are entrances everywhere, but it is particularly easy to pass between dimensions in this energy field. Higher dimensional beings can come down and we can go up through this concentrated vortex energy. The frequencies have been gradually increased so that everyone within a 50-mile radius is affected. If you are committed to personal and planetary ascension, Sedona is the fast track to "heaven."

Jananda
(Jørgen Kørsholm)
Intergalactic Communicator and Healer

I was drawn to come to Sedona by spiritual guidance. I felt I was told that I should come here to assist and help someone already living here. When I came here the first time for a visit in 1988, I was greeted with the words from White Eagle Spirit: "Welcome home, my son." Little did I know then that I would come back to the USA from Denmark and later come to this beautiful place on Planet Earth to live here.

Sedona has affected me in many ways. I see Sedona as a kind of Spiritual University where you can be taught the lessons of your life, a place where you automatically will be exposed to high-power energy from the vortex areas which will assist you and speed up the process of spiritual unfoldment.

I see many people come to this area for a period of time and then have to leave because they have processed the necessary change in their attitude.

I feel that Sedona attracts so many New Age people because this is the planet's new ascension chamber serving its purpose: assist people and the planet in the ascension process. The planetary ascension seems to me to be a natural process which is bringing more Light to the planet, and Planet Earth must follow the other planets in this galactic process.

There are actual cosmic crystals implanted in Cathedral Rock which is the planet's ascension chamber.

Karl Eymert
Naturalist, now working
as transformational guide
and counselor

In reviewing the events that changed my life so that I eventually ended up in Sedona, I feel that it probably all started with letting go of my 27-year marriage and what seemed like a secure life-long job.

I left the nest for good when I joined the Peace Corps and went to Latin America in 1984.

Working and living with indigenous people in the Americas altered my concept of myself and the world around me. I was a changed man when two years later, I returned to the United States seemingly homeless and with few possessions.

In 1987, while driving from California to New Mexico, I briefly stopped in Sedona, Arizona.

I felt an immediate attraction to the majestic beauty of the land. I liked the atmosphere of peace and tranquility which felt so healing to me.

Falling in love with Sedona was a gradual thing. I visited Sedona from California several times before finally deciding that I wanted to live here. When the decision was made, there was a job as well as a place to live in Sedona.

In the time that I have been here, I've come to learn much about the land around Sedona. I have come to love Sedona, and I feel very much at home here — probably more so than any other place I've lived before.

My life in Sedona since 1987 has been a series of inner-growth experiences and transformations which continue to this day.

I keep learning more about myself, more about the purpose of life here on earth — all life — all creation. There are growing pains associated with this process, including a good amount of frustration and confusion. However, I seem to have an inner courage and strength that continue to help me break through some difficult issues.

Whatever is mysterious about the red rock country called Sedona seems to be related to the mystery surrounding myself as a human being here on Planet Earth.

The more I discover about the magic of this land, the more I seem to discover about the magic of my beingness. One goes with the other. There is a connection, and I'm beginning to understand the meaning of the Native American affirmation, "All My Relations."

Daniel J. Borich
Bartender

At the age of 31, after reaching a point of completion in my life in Portland, Oregon, I joined the army for four years and was stationed in Korea and Colorado. About 18 months before my enlistment time was up, when I realized that I was not going to be a "lifer," a channel in Portland suggested that I visit Sedona to experience the energy of the vortexes. I was very skeptical of any such purported energy; however, that seed she planted actually manifested as a visit to Sedona three months later.

The channel, Diane Warren (who later became a dear friend), through her guidance identified as Ramas, gave specific details for my first trip to Sedona: go to the Coffee Pot Restaurant and ask for "Tom." Lacking the courage to do this, I waited until Diane took a group down to Sedona for a week. As fate would have it, Tom turned out to be the guide for our group.

When Tom took us hiking out by Bell Rock, I was suddenly struck by an overwhelming feel of "home." I turned to Diane and shared my feelings even though I didn't know quite how to define them. It was as if I had seen and experienced this land and these rocks before but couldn't place how or when. It was like a dream.

From that point on, every four to six months, I'd be drawn back to Sedona. I always had a sense of upliftment, excitement and freshness when I was here. Life suddenly became the adventure I had been seeking when I joined the army; therefore, it was not hard to decide to move here when my enlistment was up in April, 1989.

During the next year, my savings dwindled, and I was giving serious thought to going into the airline industry which would have meant moving away from Sedona. At the same time, my housemate suggested that I attend an Angelic Reunion in Tucson in May, 1990. Little did I realize how eventful that reunion would be. It turned out that I met many who would be lifelong friends including the angel of my dreams — my future wife. We now live together in Sedona. The airline dreams have flown away and I am content with my job at Enchantment Resort in Boynton Canyon. We go hiking in the canyon as often as possible, savoring the beauty, the quiet and the peace.

My (soul) mate and I have remembered two lifetimes in Sedona together. The first actually marked our initial visit to the planet in ships. The second was as American Indians living in the area of West Fork in Oak Creek Canyon. This would account for the feeling of "home." I also had the memory of being a priest in the Lemurian Temple of "New Life" located in what is now know as Boynton Canyon. It was my service to assist others to release negative energies and prepare them for their spiritual transformation.

After living in Sedona for the past three years, I *know* that the energies are *real*, powerful and transforming, and I am grateful to be a part of the focus of Light for the incoming New Age. If and when the call comes to move elsewhere, it will be part of my service to the planet to take this wonderful energy, the peace and focus that Sedona represents, and share it in my own quiet way with the world.

Carlos Warter, M.D.
Ph.D., Psychiatrist, Author
President, The World Health
Foundation for Peace

(Dr. Warter is the author
of ten spiritually based books
in Spanish and English.)

I felt guided to establish myself and my family in Sedona in order to create a base for spiritual attunement and growth. When I first visited the area, it felt deeply known to me, as if the energy field created here was in deep resonance with my soul's memory. I felt a sense of both novelty and familiarity. Sedona seemed to be a center from which I could replenish myself and therefore emanate values that are needed and wanted for global well-being, as if a Temple for Spiritual Etheric teaching already existed here.

I experience the quality of an interdimensional consciousness. Living in the Sedona vibratory field with its heavenly sightings, magnetic ley lines and peace encourages the expansion and sharing of these perspectives.

Beyond metaphysical phenomena, the anchoring of fifth-dimension perceptions and radiation here has expanded my ability to contact a larger planetary audience.

Red rocks, magnetism, crystals and interdimensional perception draw to Sedona spiritual beings who are ready for a transmutational shift in their consciousnesses. That enables the grids to become more permeable to higher frequencies, thus influencing those whose ultimate purpose is the awakened empowerment of love in the human race.

Betty Tanner

Sedona. How that word rang in my head. In the latter part of 1987, little did I know how my life would change over the next five years and what a vital part Sedona would play in it.

I knew virtually nothing about Sedona except that it was in Arizona, a state "out West." I grew up in a small town in North Carolina and after I was married, I moved to Florida. I had not travelled much out of the South so you can imagine my surprise at being drawn westward.

As the call to Sedona became stronger, I laughingly told my family and friends, "If I fall off the face of the earth, I will be in Sedona, Arizona." At the time, everyone assumed it was a phase and would pass. In many ways, I guess I, too, wanted to believe this, but the little voice inside kept calling.

During this time I had begun my spiritual unfoldment, or awakening, and was taking courses in Cassadaga, Florida, a spiritualist community near my home. I began studies in the psychic field and for the next four years I studied and became a practicing medium on a part-time basis. My full-time job was as a loan officer in a local bank. At this point, with a family, a full-time job and a weekend job doing my mediumship, I stayed quite busy. However, the call to Sedona still persisted.

In early April of 1991, I received a call from my sister Doris of Charlotte, North Carolina. She wanted to know if I would like to be in Sedona for my birthday on the 21st of April. She had a convention in Phoenix and would I fly out and meet her there. Needless to say, I was overcome with excitement. Somehow, I knew my life was never to be the same.

As I drove up from Phoenix alone to Sedona on April 21, 1991, I cried, partly because I had never traveled this far alone partly because somehow I knew that Sedona was going to help create great changes in my life. As I drove through the Village of Oak Creek and into Sedona, I experienced, as I am sure everyone must, the incredible beauty. Upon arriving in Sedona, I knew I was home. Here was a beauty and a serenity that I could enjoy for a lifetime.

Later in the day, I went on a vortex tour. When all of us in the group were on the red rocks at the Cathedral Rock Vortex, our tour guide, Bob, took us through a beautiful guided meditation. I experienced many wonderful things, especially when I saw one of my spirit guides who said, "Everything will be okay; now you have made it, you are home." At the end of the meditation, my spirit guide showed me a gift which was for me. This gift was a beautiful star, and I understood, for this meant that it was time for me to reach for "my star." Later, as the tour ended and everyone wished me a happy birthday, I told them, "By my next birthday, I will be living in Sedona." This was truly a birthday I would never forget.

My return to Florida meant many things for me. My husband, whom I had been married to for almost 25 years, and I had been having problems for some time and I knew he was not happy about my making this trip, so I had much apprehension about the future as I made the return trip.

After I arrived home the situation went from bad to worse and on June 20, 1991, after 25 years of marriage, I was on my own. Moving from a large home to a small apartment and being alone and on my own for the first time since I was nineteen created much uncertainty in my life. My children were grown, one off to college and one soon to go into the military. It was now time to learn about me!

In October of 1991, I felt the need to come back to Sedona for another visit before making the final decision to move here. I think I needed to make sure that everything I had felt while in Sedona in April had really happened and wasn't just a dream. In the meantime, I kept meeting people in Florida who had been to Sedona and who understood how I felt about the beauty and serenity. It was as if the whole world was awakening to Sedona.

My cousin Mary flew out with me in October. She, too, was overwhelmed by the beauty and could only say, "Betty, I can truly understand now your desire and need to be in Sedona." I spent a lot of time looking for a job while here but with little luck. Time after time I was told of the low pay scale, the economy and how I would be giving up a good job with great benefits if I left Florida. Much to think about for the stable, hard-working Taurus that I am.

As I left Sedona on that October morning, I stopped by the Chapel of the Holy Cross to light a candle. I envisioned this light burning until I returned. I suppose it was as if I was leaving a little of me here, as a beacon, until my return!

Yes, I returned to Florida with much to think about. I had become an avid walker in the interim. It was therapy in some way, as I was working through much in my life at that time. Florida is not known for having many hills, but I found the largest "hill" near my little garage-apartment and walked it several times each day on my daily three-mile walk. People in the neighborhood would ask, "Why do you walk up and down the same hill so often?" and I would explain that I was moving to Sedona, Arizona, and I had to get in shape for my planned hiking there. I had never hiked in my life but knew from within that this was to become a vital part of my life.

Finally around the middle of March, 1992, after *much soul searching*, I made the decision with total trust in the Infinite Spirit (God) that this was the right move for me. I gave notice at my job, told my friends and family good-bye and with the help of my wonderful daughter and a few friends, packed my belongings in my car and drove out of Florida, crying much of the way for the past, for the good times, the bad times and for a part of me that I was leaving behind.

I headed across the country with my sister Doris who had graciously agreed to ride out with me and fly back after helping me to get settled. Three days were spent on I-40, the highway that never ends! We arrived in Sedona on April 9, 1992. The voice could stop now, as I was home! No place to live and no job, virtually alone, but remember, I came on trust!

I found a place to live within two hours of my arrival and a job within eleven days. I have made many new and wonderful friends. I have hiked every weekend since my arrival. I work at Light Technology/Mission Possible, the company that prints the book that you are now reading. I have met so many people with the same beliefs as mine and so many with similar stories about how we were called to Sedona.

Sedona has truly helped in my spiritual awakening, due to the vortex energy, and it has speeded up processing for me: learning to let the past go with love and learning to create my own new reality; learning to go within and listen to that still small voice; but most importantly, learning to love myself, to feel good about me and to reach out for my own empowerment.

For many years I'd known that I could make a difference in the world but everyone would say, "You are only one person, you can't make a difference." In Sedona I have learned that I can and do make a difference each day. As we awaken to the power of love and light, we reach out and share these beautiful ideas with others and they, in turn, reach out and share. It goes on and on. The love and Light spread out to the world, changing the world by raising the vibrational level and, in turn, creating a positive, enlightening shift which allows an abundance of love and Light to go forth!

My connection to Sedona also relates to my Native American heritage. For after some past-life-regression work, I have learned that I spent at least two past lifetimes in this part of the country. The Native Americans have a wonderful respect for the energy that permeates Sedona. I only pray that everyone here, including us, the new arrivals, and those yet to come will value and honor this respect and continue to help to maintain the beauty of Sedona.

We who have been called to Sedona have a mission to help save our wonderful world which is in great peril at this time. We must continually send the love and Light out to the universe. We are the Light beings and must awaken others to the call.

Elaine Eaglewoman
Intuitive Counselor

It was 1989 and everything felt at a dead end. I wanted a spiritual life-style but I was caught up in a California yuppie fast-track. Although I was a part-time psychic reader, my own direction was foggy to me and I didn't know communities like Sedona existed.

After an unexpected layoff, I simply gave up and asked God to show me my path. Then, I just *happened* to go to work for a metaphysical magazine, that *happened* to do a feature article on Sedona, *and* a former roommate just *happened* to move there. When the photographer showed me his pictures of the red rocks, I suddenly had to go to Sedona immediately. After months of struggle, everything fell smoothly in place for me to go.

My visit to Sedona was a revelation. For the first time in my life, I felt like I'd come home. People I met knew I'd caught "red rock fever," but the possibility of moving here wasn't seriously considered until I got back to California. My roommate told me she'd dreamed I moved to Sedona. Even my mother knew about my moving before I told her. The house I had been renting had been quickly sold and I had to move, which I had strangely postponed until I came back from my trip to Sedona. Now I know why!

When I was walking down from the Kachina Woman red rock formation in Boynton Canyon after a deep meditation, I nearly stepped on a brand new, shiny copper bracelet. I was excited because I knew the metal was useful for cleaning toxins from the body, which was exactly what I needed. I was also aware I was supposed to keep it for only a short time.

Three days later, I was impulsively drawn to some Indian ruins near Loy Butte. I hadn't brought any offerings with me, but I asked the spirit-keepers if I could take a small rock as a memento. They said yes, but I had to leave the bracelet in exchange. I responded negatively because I was proud of how it had been gifted to me, so I decided a prayer would be good enough. As I finished what I thought to be a resounding blessing, my bracelet suddenly fell off my wrist. It had to be unclasped, so I was very surprised it came off. I got the message and promptly left the bracelet in a spot that I was guided to.

Sedona is a mystical and healing place because of the Earth energies generated by the red rocks and unusual formations. I feel that certain terrains are life-enhancing and exert a subtle yet powerful effect. The unique geology and high iron content of Sedona's red rocks produce energy fields or vortexes similar to electromagnetism. All of Earth's life forms, including humans, are composed of like elements.

The native peoples recognized the special qualities of this land we now call Sedona. Many tribes came here for vision quests, ceremony and celebration. Sacred burial grounds are located here as well. This land was considered too sacred to live on. Permanent dwellings were usually located on the outskirts. (*Author's note:* Elaine has an Apache ancestry.)

Nowadays with our artificial environments, pollutants and separation from nature, we become imbalanced. Power places such as Sedona help to recharge our batteries and bring us a sense of well-being. Even those no longer sensitive to Earth energies are affected by the beauty of the red rocks.

El David Shackelford
Channeled Writing

I first came to Sedona on vacation because the name had been coming to my attention in printed material, on TV and in conversations with friends and acquaintances. While watching the sunset from the Airport Mesa Vortex, I was moved by the beauty of Sedona and empowered by the high energy level here. I had a long talk with God right on the spot and said that if it was in divine order, I wanted to live here. From there, all the pieces just fell in place and six weeks later I left Cincinnati, Ohio, and became a resident of Sedona.

While I loved the New-Age community here, I had a very strong sense that the energy vortices of the areas were exactly what I needed to help me move into the next phase of my spiritual work. I had been involved in metaphysical activities for 20 years, including doing past life hypnotic regressions, teaching various classes, leading a Course in Miracles and Master Mind Classes and serving as the Spiritual Leader of Unity In Christ Church in Monroe, Ohio, for two years. However, I did not feel guided to become involved in similar activities in Sedona and for a time I could not identify why.

One month after relocating, I was writing in my daily journal when I began channeling a message from a group energy that identified itself as Your Loving Friends in Spirit. The first message was five pages long and spoke to me of the work I was to do. It said I had grown to the point where the blueprint of my life that had been created by me, the Father and the heavenly hosts before I came into physical form could now be shared with me. Much of the writing speaks of the coming changes in the Earth and the part the Light workers will play in the transformation.

Three months after the writings started, a friend showed one of them to Susie Konicov, the publisher of Connecting Link Magazine in Alto, Michigan. She asked to see more, and they are now a regular feature of that publication. While I feel very blessed to be able to bring these messages to the world, I know Sedona's energy is continuing to work with me and I'm looking forward to see what wondrous surprise will unfold in my life next.

It's said that Sedona's energy will cause whatever it is you need to work on, to be in your face. That means it will loom so large in your life that you have to deal with it. That has been happening to me, and I've been working on converting the stumbling blocks in my life into stepping stones. This includes things from this life or any past life that are unresolved. The process seems to be purifying certain individuals for elevated levels of spiritual work.

To me, the main calling card of Sedona is the energy vortices. The energy here is so high that it enables one to do things that would seem impossible elsewhere. Experts tell me the normal vortex is 50 miles across but Sedona's is only 10 miles across and is much more concentrated because of that. The rocks here are red because they contain iron oxide, a good conductor of energy. Plus, you have water springs coming from within the earth and water is also a good conductor. However it gets to the surface, it is a powerful force for good and great aid to those individuals striving to unfold their higher selves.

Janean Shaffar
Store Manager

I visited Sedona for the first time years ago and felt a synchronizing with the Earth and the energies here. My stay was brief — two or three days — but the impact was long-lasting. I kept coming back. Just to be here was enough for me.

Eventually a friend of mine was offered the opportunity to buy a shop here in Sedona. She asked me to come with her and help with the shop. I said "yes!!" in a heartbeat.

This meant I was leaving family, children and grandchildren, many long-held friendships and a life I was used to and comfortable with. But living in Sedona — making it my home — was a dream come true. I prepared to leave the mid-west and venture into an area where I knew I could create a way of life that was right for me.

My spiritual growth had reached a plateau and I knew from my previous visits that this was the right environment for further understanding and awareness. All my instincts said, "Go!" So here I am.

There have been many positive influences and events for me here in Sedona. All symptoms of a very serious, even life-threatening disease have disappeared. My awareness of the power of a positive approach in my everyday life has been greatly enhanced.

Outshining all of these, though, is an experience with a life form not of Mother Earth. A few months ago I woke up in the middle of the night with a driving need to go outside. Waking during the night is very unusual for me, but I slipped on a robe and went out into my back yard. The air was cold and crisp, the sky clear and filled with stars. I noticed a very bright star above Bell Rock. Although not an astronomer, I do have basic knowledge of the stars, but I couldn't figure which star this could be. As I stood there thinking and looking, the star split apart into two stars of the same brilliance. These two stars began moving across the sky vertically and horizontally, keeping the same distance from each other, as if mirroring each other. My logical mind kept trying to find reasons but soon figured the only explanation was the "unknown." These stars were getting closer to me and there appeared to be colors coming from them. First they were white-gold then blue, green, red, purple — all the colors of the rainbow. In all honesty, I was stunned. I have never conceived of anything as beautiful as this, yet so simple: spheres of light changing colors while moving rapidly across the sky. They finally came to rest in mid-air about 50 feet away from me.

As I stared at them, the colors kept changing and feelings came over me. Somehow, I knew we were communicating through the colors. A blue color told me they were peaceful and I felt no fear at all, just a sense of understanding.

Since I have been blessed with the ability to see auras. I knew these colors and the feelings associated with them. I used color to communicate back. It felt natural and instinctual for me, as if I were finally "talking" in my fullest capacity. As they approached, I lifted my arms out in front of me and turned my palms up — no explanation for this, I just did it — and they came to rest on my palms. The wonder of this humbled me and tears flowed. The colors lifted from my palms and told me they had to go. I cried with longing to go with them, so I asked to be taken along. Rainbows of colors flowed from the beautiful, peaceful, understanding life forms as they explained that it wasn't my time to leave and that I would be coming "home" soon enough; that I must fulfill my obligations here on Earth: and that we would "talk" many times while I remain here. Although sad, I understood exactly what they meant.

Now, when my friends laugh and lovingly call me "a star-child," I feel honored. I *am* a starchild.

There is a feeling of family among the people here. Indian tradition teaches that we are all one — not only the people, but the Earth, plants and animals, as well. All life forms are honored and respected — frivolous destruction is not acceptable. Through awareness of the needs of others our own needs are met. Respect for life coupled with joy is a very powerful combination.

For reasons I don't understand, these red rocks do emit energy, and since energy is neutral in its intent, we are responsible for the use of it — negative or positive. As those of us who are here become clearer in our intent for the use of these energies, vortexes and spiritual understandings, we become better able to attract to ourselves that which is for the highest good. Since news travels fast, many people from all over the world are hearing about Sedona.

The mysterious energy is Mother Earth herself. The mystical awareness is the ability to tap into this energy. The magic is how we use this energy and awareness to create positive influences in our lives. Spirit has given us the gift of free will. This means we can create our lives the way we want them to be which is an awesome responsibility and a humbling reality.

Helga
Kueppers Morrow
Artist / UFO Researcher /
"Quantum Time Traveler" /
Psychic / Ordained Minister /
Writer and Lecturer

We were on a spiritual quest, a long journey from the Mediterranean to Egypt. We prayed and meditated for over six hours in the Great Pyramid of Giza. After a vivid, unforgettable vision that I had while lying in the ancient sepulchre, I awakened to a mysterious encounter with five leathery, copper-skinned, wrinkled old men clothed in white robes, each with matching white turban. I believe they were high priests. We exchanged surprised glances and mentally assessed the situation as a "Quantum Time Leap." Actually I had slipped into another dimension. They remained there for a few seconds until they "fizzled out" a little bit, then disappeared. As I left the sepulchre, I knew instinctively I had been momentarily transported through time and space as we know it.

Many magical moments occurred in Egypt, but one of the most memorable took place in a 2,000-year-old Coptic church. An unexplained essence of roses wafted around us as we knelt to pray. The little monk in the church was so awed by the presence of roses around us that he asked to give us communion. This has happened to me on many occasions and has been witnessed by close associates. (Therefore I never wear rose perfume; mine is always supernatural.) The aroma of roses became so strong around me on the airplane that the man in back of me asked if I used "room spray." Again, in a hall in Cairo it happened, and even now when there is an affirmation of my life by my guides, rose scent appears as a celebration, a stamp of approval from them.

Painting by Helga Morrow

Experiences in Egypt actually led me to Sedona. The terrain of the Valley of the Kings is almost an exact duplicate of Boynton Canyon. I asked our Moslem guide, "Where in the U.S.A. is there a place like Egypt? Someone in our group responded, "Sedona, Arizona!" The rest is history.

We went home to Ohio, ran a thorough check on Sedona in the library, friends who had traveled here, and got our first brochures through The Center for the New Age.

We arrived in Sedona on Easter, 1991, with my paintings and hopes and aspirations. We stayed for a magical week during which I was inundated by visions, many of them witnessed by the dear friends we've since made in Sedona. My entities, male voices, have been witnessed by others. My mouth is tightly shut and I am fully conscious while they speak. On this occasion, they said, in loud refrains, "We'll take care of you, we'll take care of you, we'll take care of you!" Three white-robed individuals bathed in brilliant white cosmic light from the waist up were visible, then faded away. That was our message to stay in Sedona!

Ever since we moved to Sedona, my psychic experiences have been on "Fast Forward." I have had hundreds of true psychic experiences since the age of two (see "The Sedona Chronicles" which I write for the *Sedona Journal of Emergence!*), and they are too numerous to mention here. However, in Sedona my experiences occur almost daily! Sedona has given me the opportunity to expand my consciousness to such an extent that I now refer to myself as "The Quantum Time Traveler"(c), a phrase I have coined because that is exactly what I do. My entity, who has been with me since the first grade, has been a "regular" in my psychic episodes here in Sedona. He is male but androgynous with blue-eyes and blond hair parted in the middle, wearing a glittery white jumpsuit with a large reversed triangle on the chest (See painting). He has shown me underground alien installations here in Sedona. He has also shown me exact locations on maps of Earth changes, not only in Sedona, but all over the U.S.A. My rapport has been so great with this alien, this benevolent cosmic entity, that he has influenced me to become an ordained minister, and I am currently working on my Ph.D. here in Sedona. In my lectures I have given hundreds of people hope and a great deal of love which has emanated from the information I have received from him. He has "fine-tuned" my "frequency" in order to sharpen my psychic abilities, giving me an advantage I never thought possible.

Everybody comes to Sedona for a different personal reason, yet, in this tapestry of thought about Sedona, the "weaver of magic" designed surprising similarities. I phase in and out of many dimensions, yet I come back to reveal the exact truths I am given. I am becoming a finely honed vehicle for the extraterrestrials. I have gone so far as to create the first annual Sedona UFO/ET Conference & Science Expo so that people from all over the world can share in their message. I am only one small human instrument and we all have divine "appointments" with our destinies, but if my entities will allow me to share my experiences worldwide, I know deep in my heart all things are possible. If I focus on divine love and truth and always keep ego out of the way I know that what they say is true: "We'll take care of you."

Come to Sedona and experience it yourself!

Rachel Stillwater
Writer

In 1982 I heard the name Sedona on a bus. I knew I had to go there. I started on my way down the California coast, but only got as far as Santa Cruz. There, I worked as a bookstore clerk, pursuing my education by reading a line from every book that fell on me off the rickety shelves in the rickety old building.

By late '89, a more and more pressing desire had come upon me to go to Sedona. When I would sit down to meditate the only thing that would come to me was an insistent chant: "Sedona, Sedona, Sedona." On the night of October 16, I was awakened by a loud, clear voice in my room — not in my dream. The voice said, "Just get your things and go." I was shocked, I was torn. But I was in such a stir that I couldn't think, let alone make a decision to go. I felt like an animal running frantically in circles. I was not accustomed to being in such a state. Only in retrospect did I understand it.

At five o'clock on October 17, I got a demanding voice in my head to take a letter to the main post office. I knew the post office was closed, but the voice was so demanding that I got up, left my downtown apartment over a flower shop and headed down Pacific Garden Mall.

At 5:04, as history has recorded, an earthquake measuring 7.1 on the Richter Scale hit Northern California with its epicenter in the Santa Cruz area. One hundred miles away in San Francisco, the World Series stopped. The freeway collapsed.

At 5:04, I was on the sidewalk in front of the old town hall when the earth started moving. As I tried to run to the center of the street to get away from falling buildings, the ground under my feet rose up and down sixteen inches and shifted and rotated in every direction. By the time I had put my foot out to step on the ground, the ground wasn't there anymore. I fell forward, step by step, to the middle of the street. Glass shattered everywhere. Buildings crumpled to the ground. The gabled window of the Cooper Building broke off and crushed a car a few feet away from me. The sound was like being on site at a train wreck: every window breaking, every beam splitting, plaster shattering off the walls, the rocks underground snapping to pieces. From what I was seeing, I wondered if whole cities were falling into the sea. Certainly, my world as I knew it was coming to an end.

When the shaking finally stopped, there was so much building dust in the air that you couldn't see your hand in front of your face. People on the surrounding hills said later that a mushroom cloud had risen over the downtown area.

When the air cleared around me, I looked down and saw in my hand a letter to Sedona, Arizona — the only one I had ever written.

Soon after, I took direction and headed to Sedona. I drove through all of Arizona in a blinding snow storm and saw nothing. I arrived in Sedona in the dark and saw nothing. When, by morning light, I first saw the majestic Red Rocks wrapped in an aura of fog and glistening with new-fallen snow, I was pitched into a deep and silent awe that is with me to this day. I had found my home — not only where I belonged, but where I was from. Maybe where all of us are from.

On the next day in my new home, I awoke but could not move. I felt like some form of energy was running up and down my body over and over again, hour after hour. This lasted two days. On the third day, I arose with an energy and clarity I had never known before. I have often since felt healing energy coming directly from the rocks. It is as clearly perceptible to me as the energy of a light bulb if you are holding your hand close in front of it. Now I often go out to the rocks and ask for this healing energy. The Light always comes.

Sandra Bowen
Psychic Consultant,
UFO Researcher,
Author: *Mysteries of the
Crystal Skull Revealed*

I've visited Sedona once a year since 1985. I would visit the vortexes, send and receive healing from them and work with the amethyst skull under Bell Rock.

During my Sedona trip in April, 1990, birds (I call them baby angels) kept flying over me telling me that I needed to move here.

I met someone who took me to the Indian ruins in Boynton Canyon. Three small clouds with rainbows coming out of them appeared in a row and a spirit appeared in front of a tree and said, "Sedona will become Tibet."

It took me until July to actually move here. Prior to that, one day I was discussing my moving to Sedona with a friend. Every time I said something, like I needed to sell my home, a bird would bump into the window and though slightly dazed would then fly away. This happened five times! They were telling me I was right.

They would also fly over me outside and say, "Move to Sedona, move to Sedona."

In July, I was literally pulled to Chimney Rock where my new Sedona home is located. Birds again flew over me and this time said, "Welcome home."

My Sedona home was waiting for me. It is right in front of Thunder Mountain at the apex of two major ley lines. There are little devas in the yard and an inner-Earth entrance by the pine tree in front.

One morning I was pulling weeds and a large gold being with a gold medallion appeared and came up to me and took me down to the inner Earth. He showed me crystal tablets and said, "This is our history. You will tell our story." He comes to me often and takes me down to the computer room where a helmet is placed on my head and I receive information.

One night a friend and I looked up at Coffee Pot Rock and saw a spirit from the Bird Tribes. He said, "This is a healing temple." Then seven interdimensional ships formed a C, which means, "You are not alone." The exact same sequence of events occurred the next night in Boynton Canyon.

My home is very active inside, as well. People have seen silver space-suited beings, angels and tall founders as portrayed in *Close Encounters of the Third Kind*.

Maya, my wonderful founder-guide, came into my life one night. I was energized beyond belief and there she was, staring at me with her big eyes.

When I'm doing my readings, people physically experience rays that are beamed from a Pleiadian ship over us and from nearby Thunder Mountain.

Periodically, a white light will come over me and I become disoriented. I lie down and I see symbols and wonderful spirits.

When a small group of people walked to the ruins in Loy Canyon, the ships appeared again and surrounded us with white light and opened our vision to the beings who reside there. I was told that the area is on a ley line with my pine tree.

The last experience that I want to share happened at Bell Rock. I told the small blue beings that I was coming and to bring the amethyst skull. When I arrived, I felt myself being pulled into Courthouse Rock. There were representatives of each of the Indian tribes in a half circle and Bird Tribe Spirits across from them. White Bear, who illustrated a wonderful book on the Hopis, was there as was the skull. He handed me a peace pipe that we all smoked.

Recently in my home, I saw a bear at my right side, then White Bear again offered me the peace pipe and we in turn smoked it.

I visited Airport Vortex the first time I came to Sedona. I saw Sedona as a crystal city very similar to those on my home planet, Uranus — and to those in my memories of Atlantis.

The crystals create a palomagnetic field which makes it possible for us to travel through all dimensions — and for paranormal events to occur with ease.

Dirk van Dijk
Scientist, Consultant, Entrepreneur

I started visiting Sedona regularly in 1970 when my grandparents retired here. Back then, Route 89A was a dirt road from the "Y" to Cottonwood. The Chapel of the Holy Cross and Slide Rock were the main attractions, and nobody had ever heard of vortexes. The reason I liked visiting the area was because the water and air were far more pure than any I'd known in southern California.

The last job I had had before moving here was at the University of California, Irvine, as a laser technician doing medical and biological research. This led to a personal study of bioelectromagnetic fields, the Earth grid and vortices. Studies in metaphysics followed soon after I left UCI in 1984, and I found myself haunting New Age bookstores. One of these became an informal meeting/meditation place for myself and three friends. During one of these meetings I mentioned Sedona and everyone seemed mesmerized. They had recently read about it in a newsletter which they showed me. There was the magic word — vortex!

I had rented a post office box during a trip here that September thinking that I might spend some time with my grandparents before they left the planet. My friends and I now had other reasons to visit Sedona. A Thanksgiving-weekend trip here yielded magic and serendipity beyond our wildest expectations. We met two Cherokee elders, a couple of internationally famous channels and many people who seemed like old friends on introduction. We were invited back to help with some research projects, plans were made and I moved here during the Christmas season of 1984. What had at first seemed to be mundane family business in Sedona had already been overshadowed by what is now an eight-year-long adventure in spiritual exploration.

Sedona has helped me most in focusing my growth through relationships of many kinds and on many levels. My background in the "hard" sciences was stretched to its limits in metaphysical research with psychics and healers in such fields as orgonomy, radionics and alchemy. The attraction Sedona has for those who are interested in such fields has created a large sub-culture of far-thinking people. This alone seems to generate an aura or attitude of ease about new ideas and individual development of an inner spiritual life. The relatively intense electromagnetic fields known to exist here seem to amplify this aura. My own out-of-body experiences, lucid dreams, psychic and intuitive development, UFO sightings and past-life remembrances were validated and supported by Sedonans with practical experience in these areas.

My knowledge in the "soft" sciences (sociology, psychology) was enhanced during years spent as manager and owner of metaphysical bookstores. The popular self-help literature provided a crash course in abused inner-child healing, AA, ACoA, and (thankfully positive) spiritual emergency/emergence. So did 25,000+ customers world-wide. I found the most effective way to help people going through the psychic and emotional roller coaster that Sedona put them through was with "hug therapy." It wasn't long before I heard this referred to as the "Sedona Handshake." It's nice to know that smiles, tears of joy (or pain) and hugs don't need translation. (As a result of my years of varied experiences, I am compiling a book which will be entitled *Union*.)

My empirical research in Sedona shows me that spirituality, metaphysics, consciousness and physics are like different notes on the musical scale of creation, all following cosmic rules of harmony. The published Earth-grid maps do not include Sedona; however, a quick look at local geography indicates abundant underground water streams. The friction of water flowing in rock produces electrical currents with circular polarization. The 4% iron oxide content in the red rocks would tend to focus the energy in a tight area. The effect this has on the human biofield depends on the strength and frequency of the field(s) involved.

The attraction energy spots on the planet have for humans is well known and prehistoric. The attraction of these particular red rocks may be far older than we think. A recent hypothesis put forth by Richard Hoagland makes at least some humans descendants of an interstellar colonization effort that first stopped on Mars. A subsequent generation that could withstand a higher gravity was then sent to Earth. Could the red rocks of Sedona be triggering a dim racial memory? Perhaps the most poetic and hopeful scenario regarding the Earth changes was put forth by Louis Malle in his teleplay *My Dinner with André*. The idea is put forth that before the planet goes through the "shake & bake" period, small groups of people will start to gather in what they psychically perceive as "safe" areas. These groups will be repositories of the arts and sciences of this civilization and rebuild the world carrying (hopefully) only the best forward. Sedona seems to be just such a place. So, welcome home, again.

Alana Marie Davis
Psychospiritual Counselor,
Flower and Gem Essence
Therapist, Co-creator
of Celestial Life Elixirs

I was rather oblivious to the metaphysical stature of Sedona when I moved here seven years ago. I had known the area since childhood, and my father had planned to retire here before his death retired him elsewhere. A friend moved to Sedona and titillated me with stories of the beauty and power. After a single visit to my friend, a matter-of-fact knowingness persuaded my move. I experienced an uncanny ease in the move, details effortlessly falling in place, the next step in my life presenting itself very distinctly, but with little fanfare.

Since my arrival in Sedona, my personal awakening process has accelerated tremendously. It has been a grand and endless spiritual adventure with remarkable experiences that would take chapters to highlight. Certainly my intuitive faculties have sharpened; past-life remembrances and higher-consciousness experiences have become a virtual everyday occurrence. Exceptionally vivid access to the subconscious realms of experience have opened for me here and gradually my super-conscious, conscious and subconscious levels of mind are merging into a unified experience.

Of crucial importance have been the connections made in Sedona with certain individuals with whom I am deeply aligned on spiritual planes. Internally and externally, relationships have grown to an amazing depth and love. Would this all have happened just the same in Wichita, Kansas? I suspect not....

In my perception, Sedona is both a gathering place and a springboard for many people whose purpose deals in one way or another with the awakening of the Earth. I find Sedona to be both magnetic and stimulating, and utterly demanding of the spiritual seekers who arrive here to face their shadow and claim their truth. It is both the most wondrous and exciting place I have ever lived and the most challenging. I believe (although I have no concrete evidence), that there are energetic devices (a spaceship?) buried in the Earth under Sedona and energies directed to Sedona from extraterrestrial sources that do, indeed, make Sedona energetically powerful and unique.

Mason P. Rumney III
Energy Consultant

I was drawn to Sedona for basically esthetic reasons. I was searching for a warmer climate and for an open, and beautiful desert area. I love to hike and be in nature. Hiking brings to me a balance of body, mind and spirit. The desert aids in my thought processes — I see and hear things more clearly, and this brings me to a joyous state of being. I was also looking for a place to build my dream house. I located and purchased a parcel of remote desert property west of Sedona. I built a large dome house which has gained a lot of publicity because of its unique design and energy-conserving qualities. I am now in the business of selling and constructing dome houses. I have made my desert dome house self-sufficient, complete with its own windmill-powered well and solar panels for my other electrical needs.

Being in Sedona has affected me in a number of ways. I have had visual experiences with "The Ancient Ones" as I camped in high and remote Indian ruins near my home. It was on one of these camping trips that we watched a UFO flying far below us, and it disappeared right into the side of the mountain. Quite a spectacle to behold!

I have learned that we are in a co-creation. We have a responsibility to our physical world which interacts with our infinite spirit worlds.

Sedona is renowned for its abundance of spirit-oriented experiences. I have come to the conclusion that the truth of spirituality will always be mystical to those who have a purely logical perspective. I firmly believe that there are those who have gone beyond our present physical state of living. And that is hopeful indeed.

Sunshower
Portrait Artist, Writer, Clown, Mime

I first learned of Sedona through a book in which it was mentioned only once. My research into this spiritual haven piqued my curiosity enough to spur me to action. Hence, my initial "visitation." As with most people, once the vibration has been established, it is all but impossible "never" to return. After my second visit, I received through my telepathic writings a message that predicted a rather sudden move from my environs. Also, the piece of art I call *Stepping Out* was produced that same month. Five months later, I found myself living in Sedona. A strong urge to understand more about Native Americans had risen in me. Additionally, a passion to be close to the Earth Mother was overwhelming. The first place I stayed was near Loy Butte, a ranch with no lavatory facilities. I became very close to Mother, as I communed with her in my daily physiological necessities. I am living proof that one ought to be careful about one's wishes!

Besides the increased nocturnal "visitations," visions and lights in my room, my writings have become more intense since moving to Sedona. I have even been encouraged to publish them. What's more, my creativity has sprung up in so many directions that I am still boggled. A doorway which I will call Stage Presence has swung wide open. As predicted by my writings in May of 1987, "...future, yet-masked situations...beckon to (my) creativity." Until May, 1988, I had never even been on a stage. And now, it seems this is where my calling is, as in "my mission." I feel that healings take place within my audiences on levels that are not obvious, but rather unseen.

What I *do* see is that Sedona's own energy has struck a chord deep within me that has turned itself inside out, and now rings out through me. It is a child-like vigor with which I explore aspects of myself I would never have dreamed about in my "other life" — that is, pre-Sedona. I now consider myself to be multi-dimensional. In fact, I have advertised myself as such, in appropriate places, of course. Here are a few examples of my new-found avenues of expression:

Art concerts that blend art, music and dance — comedy — mime — clowning — singing (in concert, at parties and public functions) — the combination of miming and caricaturing — theatrical performance.

Being first a portrait artist, it is natural for me to use this expression about Sedona: "One comes face to face with oneself here." The fact that the faces of the red rocks appear to shift so drastically with the climatic, solar and lunar changes is only another symbolic indication that something poignant goes on in this place. The initial step is awareness. Then allowance. Then the fun begins, and I use that term loosely. It really take a great deal of perseverance to stay in Sedona *because* of its intense energy. One's integrity is truly put to the test here. When you choose Sedona, you have reached the point of no return ... and who'd want to, anyway?

Coming to Sedona is like taking a magical mystery tour. You feel you have "come home" when you arrive. People you meet seem familiar to a lesser or greater degree. I strongly feel the oceanic qualities, probably because of the seven times that Sedona has been submerged. Again, my writings inform me that I (am) assisting people into their Light Bodies — as I did in Atlantis — via "the rearrangement of molecular structure in an underwater setting." I believe the H_2O energies are alive and well here...and will become physically manifest once more by the first decade of 2000 A.D.

Stepping Out, by Sunshower

Ron Babin
Healing Massage and Nutrition

I went to Santa Fe to visit a healer friend of mine with the intention of moving there. At the time I was not working as a healer but as a chef (for 21 years) and years as a massage therapist (for 10 years). I was also an avid yoga practitioner, had been meditating regularly for 25 years, and for 7 1/2 years co-owned a natural-health food store and restaurant in New Orleans.

I fell in love with Santa Fe, but my friend told me upon my arrival there that she was moving to Sedona. I asked where it was and she told me, "Arizona." I replied, "Arizona! There's nothing there but the Grand Canyon and desert!"

She insisted I see the place before judging and the next day we set off for Sedona. The drive through the Painted Desert and Petrified Forest was a breathtaking experience. I couldn't imagine anything being more beautiful. Unfortunately we arrived in Sedona at night so I did not get to see the incredible sights in a Sedona morning.

The next morning I was the first to rise, so I did my yoga and meditation as best I could in the cramped room that my 14-year-old son, my friend Elizabeth and I were sleeping in, then I went for a walk.

I couldn't believe my eyes or my senses. I stopped, frozen in my tracks, and spun around. Everywhere I looked was red-rock beauty, rock formations that made me feel as though I'd landed on another planet. This was truly like nothing I'd ever seen or even dreamed of, in my life.

During the day we hit all the metaphysical hot spots, the vortexes. We arrived in Boynton Canyon last and decided to meditate there. We were all practicing the T.M. technique at that time. We found an Indian ruin in a little cave for our meditation. I found a nice flat rock to sit on and was able to cross my legs in a lotus position so I was quite comfortable.

My meditation was deep and I had visions of crystalline Indians riding horses across the deep blue sky. I was in bliss. Then something strange happened. I felt as though the rock and I were rising. Since I had been given the flying technique in the T.M. program eight years earlier, nothing like this had ever happened. I did not want to open my eyes for fear of losing the sensation. When the time finally came for me to open my eyes, I was staring at the opposite wall! I shouted out, "Elizabeth, the earth moved!"

She opened her eyes to look and both of us witnessed the fact that I had done some movement, with the rock under me. Elizabeth simply stated, "Well, some people fly around on carpets. You just did it on a rock."

To say the least, I was ready to move to Sedona. My next trip there, I decided to spend the night in that same cave in the ruins. None of my friends wanted to go with me, so I went alone. Since I had only been there once before, I had some difficulty finding the cave, but once I did, I set up my sleeping bag and accessories in the ruin. I did my yoga as best I could on the very hard, rocky surface, then meditated with the hope of levitating even higher and longer than the first time.

Nothing happened except that I had a very deep and long meditation. Since I did not know the area well, I assumed that the loud noises which sounded like a dozen Mack trucks above my head must be a highway. From the cave I could see what I thought were headlights shooting out. The noise lessened after about 15 minutes, and I gazed at the incredible blanket of stars that filled the dark sky.

I began to get sleepy and, since I had a job interview in the morning, I decided to strip and climb into my sleeping bag. I felt a presence around me but thought it was only my guides blessing me for coming back to this sacred land. I fell asleep very peacefully.

After about three hours, I awoke. There was a strange but calm feeling in the air. The stars were like glitter in the sky. I wondered what the time was and struck a match to look at my watch. The pitter-patter of little feet on the outside of the wall of the ruin forced me to jerk my body straight up. It was not the sound of an animal's feet at all, but more like the sound of a three-year-old bare-foot baby.

I freaked and gathered up my things, trying to put my clothes on while running out the door of the ruin toward the path. I stopped in my tracks and felt petrified at what I saw, and didn't see. The path was nowhere in sight. Slowly, I turned around and looked up at the top of the mountain where I had heard the noise earlier. There sat a huge, dark cloud, with those bright lights shooting out of it like headlights. Chills ran throughout my body. I nearly wet my disheveled pants.

I didn't know what to do. I panicked searching for the path. It was so dark I couldn't find it. I looked up at the sky and with a loud voice shouted, "Oh God, what am I to do?"

An equally loud voice came back to me. "Go back!" was all it said. I don't know why I obeyed, but I returned to the ruin, laid all my things out again, got undressed and crawled into my sleeping bag. I closed my eyes and began meditation in the hope of falling into a deep sleep until morning. Instead, I relived a past life.

I felt and saw myself in the womb. I experienced the whole birth process and each year as I grew to be a young teenaged Indian boy. I and others my age were put in charge of watching the Chief's tent while the men went off to hunt. Our camp was raided by another tribe and I was killed by a spear that went into my stomach.

I awoke from this nightmare with excruciating pains in my stomach. I felt as though I were going to vomit. I drank some water, for I was sweating and very warm. When I went outside the ruin, cautiously, I found the temperature to be very cool. The ruin had no roof, so I was puzzled by this. When my stomach felt better I returned to my hard bed in the hope of falling into another sleep as peaceful as the first one had been.

Meditation came easily and once again put me into a deep experience of yet another past life. I went through the whole birth process again, living each year as though it were actually happening I was an Indian again, about 26 this time. I was male, a warrior, and getting ready to set off to fight. During the battle, I was killed by an arrow to my heart.

Once again, I awoke in excruciating pain. I was certain that a heart attack was taking place and I would not make it through the night. I gasped and drank water, crawling at the same time out of the ruin into the cool night, or mid-morning. I had no idea of the time for I was fearful of striking a match again.

I dressed somewhat calmly, determined to get out of this place. I gathered all my belongings and headed in the direction of the path. I could not see it but knew that it was there somewhere and just started charging out into the dark trees to find it. I began sliding down the mountainside and grabbed onto something that hurt. I felt myself almost being pulled up, but there was no one there. I attributed the helping hand to my beloved guides.

I sat on a big rock and looked up at the dark cloud still perched atop the mountain, the bright lights still protruding from its rumbling mist. Again I said, almost silently this time, "God, what do you want me to do?" The answer came quickly: "Go back." I obeyed.

My body was tired, my bones began aching, I wanted so badly for morning to come. I'd nearly finished off the gallon of water I'd brought. Once again I disrobed and crawled into my sleeping bag, this time sitting up to meditate hoping that I would not have another past-life experience.

No such luck. The whole experience began again, but this time I was female. I grew to be an Indian woman in my early sixties. The Spaniards had conquered most of the land and enslaved my people. I was a housekeeper of sorts, in charge of the children, as well. I was trying to get the children into the hacienda for dinner and the master of the house saw me patting their behinds. He took out his whip. In one stroke it was around my neck and with one slight pull he broke my neck.

I came out of this nightmare the same as the others, with piercing pain, and this time I was choking so badly I emptied the water jug. I couldn't stand any more. I begged for sleep, and fell into my sleeping bag totally exhausted.

When I awoke it was still dark but there was a light in front of me, sort of hanging over the ruin about 20 feet up in the sky. It was pale blue and shimmering. Somehow I knew that was a sign that I could leave. Calmly, I packed my gear, dressed and walked right to the path. Even though it was pitch dark, I found it and walked out of the canyon to the parking area.

Now, I need to backtrack a moment and tell you that when I had driven to the canyon, my car's gas tank had been empty. Not near empty, but past "E" as far as it could go. When I realized this, my heart nearly stopped. I was at least six miles out in the canyon and my gas tank was on empty. I calmed myself, closed my eyes and said in a soft breath, "I trust in God, I trust in God, I trust in God." Then I started the car and drove.

I was feeling pretty good and knew I would make it to a gas station. The canyon and its many bizarre formations were quite a sight in the dark of the night. That thick cloud with the protruding lights came into my thoughts. I tried not to think what it was, but deep in my heart I knew that it was an alien ship. I had always prided myself on believing in these things, but now that it had actually happened to me, I felt as though I'd been through hell.

The car began to bump and I thought I was out of gas. I looked out my window and saw a sign that said Sedona, eight miles, and the arrow was pointing in the opposite direction from which I was facing. I don't know why I did not panic at this point, but I didn't. I simply turned the car around and started driving, not looking at the E on the gas gauge.

Within 20 minutes, I was on the highway. I sighed heavily. Turning, I went straight to the nearest gas station. As I drove up, I noticed that every pump had an "out of order" sign on it. I sighed again, began my "Trust in God" chant and headed into town to the next nearest gas station.

When I arrived they were just opening. I got out of the car and the manager looked at me and said with an Iowa drawl, "Had a bad night, did ja?" "I got lost for awhile," I replied, "but I'm okay now." After getting gas, I headed straight to my friend's house in the hope of getting some sleep before my job interview. It was now 5:30AM. When I walked in the door the lady I'd traveled with woke up. She looked at me with shock and surprise on her face, and said, "My God, what happened to you?"

"I've been through hell," I replied, and headed for the bathroom. The friend whose house we were staying in awoke also, and when she looked at me, she made the same remark. I gave her the same reply and went into the bathroom to shower.

When I turned on the light I was immediately faced with a large mirror. In the mirror was a man with his hair sticking straight up on his head, eyes as wide as an owl's, and blood dripping down the hand that had been hurt when I had tried to escape from the canyon. I could only think of the gas station attendant. One more thing: my shoes were on the wrong feet.

The next morning my friend brought a psychic over to talk to me, since I could not tell either of my friends what had happened to me. The psychic managed to get the whole story out in detail and stopped me at crucial points to explain why I was having certain experiences. And yes, that was, in fact, an alien spaceship and the pitter-patter of little alien feet.

The psychic reminded me that the day before she had told me that three of my chakras were blocked: the solar plexus (stomach, spear), the heart (arrow) and the throat (whip). She checked them again and said they were now opened. Well, I certainly hoped so, after the hell I'd been through!

That was four years ago. Six months after that experience my son and I moved to Sedona and are living happily ever after.

Sherill L. Funk
Lecturer, Workshop Leader, Intuitive Consultant

I had lived in the Los Angeles area for many years and never thought I would leave. However, very shortly after I began channeling, I felt the urge to pick up and go somewhere. As the months went by, this urge became stronger and stronger. Even though I grew up in Tucson, I had never been to Sedona. One of the women I met in my channeling class was taking a trip to Sedona and asked if I would like to go.

In October of '85, five females piled into a small camper and off we went. Of course, I fell in love with Sedona at first sight. The spiritual energy was so very wonderful, especially compared to Southern California. We attended a workshop and meditation here and returned home.

For the next two months, I had a very difficult internal struggle as I had heard it was hard to make a living here and I wasn't sure I wanted to go back to the desert. Before making a final decision, during Christmas vacation three of us came, once again, to Sedona. It was too strong to resist. We returned to California on January 5, 1987 and by January 21 had moved into a home in Clarkdale, Arizona.

My vision was that I would be a student at the Tibetan Foundation's Temple of Light and learn from all the wonderful teachers there. Much to my surprise, within a three month period of time, I was teaching there also. What I thought was my reason for coming here wasn't the reason at all. Looking back, I feel that Sedona itself and the many people passing through here were my teachers.

It's been nearly seven years since I moved here and I've worked with all the issues I have. The energy is so intense here that I feel we all process most of the time. It soon becomes a way of life. However, I also feel that it's necessary to get away once in awhile. I've been able to take a look at myself more objectively than I feel I would have somewhere else. I've come face to face with a lot of my fears and overcome an incredible amount of negative programming about who I am. I've also watched my son deal with many of his issues, and at a much younger age than I was able to. And I've seen him heal too.

When The Center for the New Age was very young, I was one of the primary readers on staff. So often couples would come in for a reading and the first question they would ask was why they were suddenly arguing and fighting. Almost always, they had been here for about three days. What I learned was that any unresolved "stuff" would come up like clockwork between couples at about that time. I can't even imagine what it must be like, multidimensionally, for those of us who live here!

I'm now able to have total recall on past life experiences at will, when that is necessary for my process. My psychic and intuitive abilities have blossomed greatly as well. I feel that I have become much more of who I am and have cleared a pathway to do so.

Sedona has been a real blessing in that I've moved out a lot of old stuff in a very short period of time. I'm sure I'm not the only one who feels that way. Surprisingly, I also feel my time here is complete. I don't know exactly where I'll be moving on to, but I know the move is soon.

I feel that many of us have taken a sort of sabbatical from life during our stay here. And it's important for those of us who have had the opportunity to be here in this very special environment to now take what we've learned about ourselves and reintegrate back into "mainstream America" in whatever way we choose. After all, we're part of the whole, too, and our contribution is vital.

Why is Sedona a mystical place? Well, first of all, I feel that the energy vortexes have a lot to do with this mystique as no one can really explain what they do because each individual experience is unique. However, if you've ever looked at the rock here up close, you'll see these very tiny pockets. If the sun hits them just right, you can see that each of these tiny pockets has little crystals inside. There are millions of them on Bell Rock alone. When you consider that the whole area is loaded with these little pockets, you get an idea why the energy here is so accelerated.

I personally feel that this was once a sacred site at the time of Lemuria. I have seen Sedona underwater about half way to the tops of the rocks with dolphins and other sea creatures swimming in the water. I have seen priests and acolytes holding ceremony here, particularly back near Schnebly Hill and out in the Chapel area. It was obvious from what I saw that they utilized the crystalline energy for ceremonies.

Because of all the UFO activity and the many strange and bizarre things that have happened to people here, it is certainly an energetically unique place and I feel that we've only scratched the surface of what actually goes on here, externally and well as internally. I'm thankful for the time I've spent here, the many lessons I've learned but, most of all, for the people who have become my extended family. I hope that, as those of us who are called, go out to reintegrate with the rest of the world, the light that is Sedona will shine forth from the heart of each of us because I believe that our experiences here have touched us more deeply than we yet realize.

Robert T. Jaffe, M.D.
**Founder of Energy Mastery
Seminars and
the School of Energy Mastery**

In 1985, I found myself doing a survival training out in Boulder, Utah, which is about 200 miles north of Sedona. I was in the final phase of the training when an etheric being appeared to me. This was my first full clairvoyant sighting and I was shocked by the amount of color and light that was present. I was also scared, not sure whether or not it was positive or negative and what its effects on me would be. I spent the day walking around it, getting to know it, and later the energy began to communicate with me telepathically. It told me that my spiritual growth was going to take on a new phase and that I was to go to Sedona, Arizona, and begin the process of meditation and healing there; that Sedona was a very powerful place that would open up my psychic abilities and allow me to begin the ascension into higher levels of being. I had heard of Sedona, and shortly after that I flew out to Arizona and drove up to Sedona in a V.W. bus via Route 179. The moment I saw Courthouse Rock, Bell Rock and the Village of Oak Creek, I knew I had come home. I knew that Sedona was a very special place. Prior to that survival training, I had been working as a successful doctor in Hawaii making $75,000 a year by working two days a week.

When I arrived in Sedona, I knew that in order to stay here I would have to give up the easy job, the money I was making and the islands in order to live in this desert. Yet I also knew that, although it would be difficult, it would be extremely rewarding spiritually. I made the choice to stay in Sedona one day while meditating down on Lower Red Rock Loop Road. I have never regretted it.

My experience in Sedona has been incredible and I feel that it has accelerated my personal and spiritual growth by such a factor that I don't even understand the nature of it. Essentially, soon after I got to Sedona, my clairaudient and clairvoyant experiences rapidly increased. Of course, Sedona had many people already opening to these levels of being and there were a number of organizations that were teaching people to channel and to see auras. About four months after I arrived, I went through my third initiation, the soul merge. That was a significant turning point for me even though I had trouble believing it was real when it happened. About six months after my arrival in Sedona, my ability to see the colors of auras began to open. Emotionally, my life was absolutely topsy-turvy.

My feeling is that Sedona radiates such powerful energies that the pressure of these energies going from the Earth through our bodies is constantly moving us into the fifth dimension and forcing all the aspects of ourselves that are out of alignment with the fifth dimension to come up. It is not easy to live here, and in the beginning I often took sabbaticals from Sedona, about one a month. With time, it has become more comfortable for me to live here and I don't need to leave the field so often. Sedona is one of the key points on the geo-planetary grid system. My feeling, based on having traveled to many of the power places in the world, is that Sedona carries one of the highest vibrational energies on the planet and has accumulated a large amount of fifth-dimensional energy. Because of this, any human being that comes into this field, conscious or not, is going to be rapidly accelerated into the higher dimensions. Through my clairvoyant vision it's clear to me that we are living in a sort of citadel of etheric cities, both above Sedona and built into the mountains. From the perspectives of the fifth dimension and the Light frequencies, the mountains are not physical but are able to be entered into through Light. I believe that many of these mountains are cities and some of them are actually homes to the Gods. Very often as you look at the rocks, you can see the faces of many different historical figures and many powerful figures that may play a role in the future as well. So, in a way, we're living in a natural monument to the Gods and in an etheric city with so much power that it affects us in a very great way.

I feel that the center of this power is in the Boynton Canyon area and that when you go out there and follow some of the canyons in, you have reached the point of maximum acceleration. I also feel that one of the interesting aspects of Sedona is that there are crystals buried deep within the hills. I have not seen any large crystals here physically; however, when I look with my auric vision it's clear that the mountains are surrounded by a very peculiar aura. The different mountains have different colors — some of them are greens and yellows. But the quality of vibration is something different from anything I have seen around rocks other than crystals. They pulse with energy and have a particular crystalline feel to them, which is very unusual. So I think we are living in one of the very important places on Earth that at some level represents not the heart chakra, as many people think, but rather the fifth and sixth chakras of the Earth which thus resonates harmonically with our fifth and sixth chakras. I do not think that this is a seventh-chakra area.

People who want to work on the crown chakra will have to go to higher areas such as the San Francisco Peaks or the Himalayas or perhaps the Matterhorn. However, the energies in Sedona can be used to rapidly accelerate our quest toward enlightenment. By meditating in these vortex areas, particularly out in Boynton Canyon, a great deal of movement can be made in our upward ascension toward Light.

As far as the UFOs and aliens, I think that we have multiple varieties of them in this area. I do feel there is an underground base somewhere out in the canyon areas and I think that area was chosen because of the intense amount of Earth energy that is available there for those beings. They can use this Earth energy to recharge their ships and probably as a power source for their cities as well. I think there are good and bad energies out there — or shall we say pro-human and anti-human energies. I also believe that much of the UFO disharmony that we have here is actually occurring on the etheric levels, not in the physical. Most of the people in Sedona are constantly experiencing both distortion and harmony from a multitude of etheric UFO energies which are going in and out of their consciousness at night. I know that very often when I close my eyes, I am aware of hundreds of small metallic-looking, etheric ships moving in and out of my consciousness. Sometimes they throw me out of balance, although at other times there are ships that balance me. I am also aware that if I look up at the sky at night, very often I can pick out as many as ten to fifteen ships that seem to be holding stationary positions in the sky. One of the ways you can distinguish these from stars is that the ships have blinking red, blue or green lights, or a combination thereof. The red and green ones tend to be vibrating at a much lower level and the red ones are extremely negative. The blue and the blue and green ones have a very positive effect and seem to be carrying and holding a sense of balance and harmony for the people of Sedona as well as for the energy fields of Sedona.

I do feel that there are vortexes here, electrical and magnetic fields, but I think that the vortexes are different from what people think they are. For example, Cathedral Rock is a very high spiraling vortex that is probably being created by a number of very high spiritual beings that are using those rocks as their homes. The Airport Vortex for me is very different from that, I don't experience it as a spiraling vortex. What I do see when I'm meditating in that vortex are very powerful patterns of energy that seem to have been placed at the four corners at the top of the vortex so that some sort of resonant energy is being created that can be used to relax the physical body, relax the emotional body and bring in a sense of peace. At the Airport Vortex, I have had the experience, as I looked off toward Bell Rock, that there is what appears to be a twin-peaked mountain where perhaps a river carved out the center. Each time I've gone up there, I've had contact with a very powerful spiritual being who has identified himself as the Atlantean. For him to be appearing in this place makes me believe that there must still exist some powerful connections between the Atlantean energies and Sedona.

I think one of the things that we will be seeing in the future in Sedona is that the influx of people from all over the country is bringing a great deal of disharmony and control into the Sedona energy fields. So there is often what appears to be a battle between the expansive upward-rising energies and the fundamental, conservative energies that are used to keep Sedona in an old structural framework of consciousness. I think that many of the people who are coming to Sedona and are interested in vortexes, meditation and spiritual growth will do very well here, and yet they will have to be aware of the conflicts that are present within this community. They will also have to be prepared to meet with the extraterrestrial energies both on the etheric and possibly even on the physical level. It's important for them to realize that no harm can be done to them unless they invite it from within themselves and that the true healing will occur when they realize that they are free, and do not need to be controlled or dominated in any way. Each person who comes to Sedona will be stepping into a very powerful world of the unknown, and they will need to be alert and aware of the forces of energy that are present here. This is not a spiritual kindergarten, but rather a place of very advanced spiritual consciousness.

Alan Leon
Wilderness Guide —
Sedona Adventures

To the wild lands of British Columbia and Montana I had given the better half of eighteen years, years spent with nature, usually without human companions, though in prayer, certainly not alone.

One day my heart said, "Go see Arizona." So while passing through to the deep deserts the road brought to me the surprise of Sedona. Funny how the northern Rocky Mountains looked like my whole life, then "Bam!" It all turns around. A few days of meditation while camped up in Long Canyon made it clear to me it was time to move. Having been away from people long enough, it was a good time for fellowship and sharing.

Sedona is a gushing geyser of natural Earth energies. Riding these flows has helped push this life into the realms of beyond beyond and back again. A partial list of my experiences here begins with a great deepening of meditation and clarity, and hearing the still, small voice within.

Various spirit friends and guides appearing in visions impart wondrous adventures and lessons. Often I experience the great joy of being with the many nature spirits, the little ones and the larger ones too. It is so inspiring to see the bright light of angels in the sky.

Practicing pranayama, the yoga of breath, I have slipped the body's bonds and flown above these canyons, seeing the world as brighter, even more colorful and beautiful through spirit's eye. I fall into the great void between breaths and come back to find hours have passed.

I have offered love, heart to heart, in telepathic sharing beyond the need of words. I have Seen dissolved as gifts of spirit, a wondrous array of dis-eases.

Then there are all those UFOs, day and night; I experienced over a dozen sightings my first year in Sedona. Three times I saw a large, white, glowing ball descending. The last time it was in exact sync with an earthquake here. There is a dimensional doorway in a kiva, an ancient ceremony room, in a remote Sedona canyon where we've enjoyed close, touching and repeated contact with very big and different-looking beings from other worlds. The images and messages they share are inspirational.

The role I play here is that of a wilderness guide (for Sedona Adventures) for hiking, camping and questing. The great gift here is the people. I share these canyons with seekers from around the planet, such as the tourists from Manchuria and their good news of the spontaneous spiritual awakening throughout Asia; the Incan messenger from Peru who was sent to say the Age of Spirit has come; the Master of Soaring Crane from Beijing and his gift — a key to traveling to worlds beyond; the Native American woman, whose tribal tradition calls Sedona "the Gateway Between Worlds," the "going-between"; from New Zealand, the Maori called to Sedona to follow their living dreams and ancient prophesies; the woman of the Yaqui, knowing the strength of dreams. The living list still grows. It is such a delight to stand in the glow of the many pilgrims who find their seeking answered here.

In the canyons is the magic. This child has wandered in the wilderness from Alaska to Mexico and knows the feeling here to be unique, a peace all its own. There is the healing of Cathedral Rock, the sweetness of Doe Mesa. The strong spirit of Sacred (Boynton) Canyon, all those nature spirits of Loy Canyon, Vision Hill and Looking Rock. There are over 80 archeological sites — this place has been very popular in the past, too. There are the questions of the stone-built pueblos and cliff dwellers, tens of thousands of people who vanished. There are the questions of Secret Canyon: why all those black helicopters, and underground explosions?

Since ancient times people from every direction have quested to this place of the red rocks. These canyons, like old cathedrals, gather the quiet feeling of sacredness, deeping down through the mysteries of ages.

Luis A. Romero
Artist

It seems impossible that Jean and I have been residents of Sedona for only six and a half years. So much has happened in that time.... enough to fill several more years at least.

When we lived in Phoenix, we were consistently drawn to Sedona, week-end after week-end — any excuse would do — we could not stay away from the red rocks for very long. There were 'restlessness attacks' and 'anxiety attacks' in Phoenix which seems to level out into joyful, peaceful serenity and/or happy exhilaration and inspiration as soon as we were in the Sedona vicinity.

After a year or two of being Sedona visitors, and after I had taken an early retirement from Goodyear Aerospace, we talked about the possibility of living in Sedona, and a short time later we rented a lovely little place at the base of Capitol Dome for six months as trial period for residency. Six months later we were totally "hooked" on the amazing energies we experienced and the wonderful people we were privileged to know. And so we bought our home and "settled in" to the high vibrational life of Sedona.

In the years that have followed, we have had so many peak experiences, both negative and positive ones, and covering all of the physical, emotional, mental and spiritual aspects of our lives. Moderation, we find, is not one of the attributes of Sedona living, and most experiences are at a peak extreme of either the positive or the negative.

Painting by Luis Romero

I was told by my guides (of the White Brotherhood) that in Sedona I would reach the pinnacle of service in my field of talents, and this has surely seemed to be true. My illustrated readings (coupled with Jean's prose writings) have gone to clients in all parts of the U.S. and to many other countries on the planet, and the reports that come back to us are all about the great transformations and wonderful changes that have come about for those who received our work. For this we are very grateful.

I believe that Sedona has come to be known as a mystical, magical place because of the special energies which seem to speed up, or accelerate, life's events and circumstances. I agree with the many who say that the whole Sedona area is sacred ground. It is a magnificent place, imbued with the spirit energies of the Native Americans who have called it home — as well as the more ancient energies of the Atlantians and Lemurians who came here for "R and R" — restoration and rejuvenation.

We continue to stay here because we want it all — the spiritual enrichment, the restoration and rejuvenation, and the fantastic physical pleasure of being nurtured and supported by the Red Rock vibrations of Sedona.

PART 6
THREE CHANNELS

I interviewed three channels to get a
spirit's viewpoint of Sedona.

Robert Shapiro

Robert channels Zoosh,
Bearclaw, Speaks of Many Truths
and the Heart Spirit.
He has channeled many powerful
and enlightening books,
including *The Explorer Race*.

I am Speaks of Many Truths. What would you like to discuss?

Why are so many spiritual people being drawn to the Sedona area?

In terms of the people being drawn here, it is actually a two-way draw. People who are drawn to Sedona actually draw things out of Sedona that others do not feel. It is as if a person were to take a walk through an art gallery. One person would look at a picture and say, "Oh, this is magnificent. It is of such great beauty!" And another one would walk by with hardly a glance. Different energies are blessing different people. Sedona has always been a place that has magnetic, feminine and transformative energies. It is also not unlike the crystal skull, a place that retains knowledge, like a library, that can be pulled out at a future or past date, if you have the ability to travel in time. You could conceivably go over to certain rocks here in Sedona, and place — in energy form — all that you know about a certain subject into the rock for a past or future life of your own.

The entire area, then, is like a massive memory unit, so people who are drawn here on their spiritual paths feel a tremendous sense of home or familiarity. They will find themselves going to particular rock formations and having certain experiences. Very often their past or even future lives have been here and have left information, experience or feelings for them. This place is a depository, then. People who are drawn here will very often receive help from their past or future selves, or even leave memory imprints of who and what they are now to be retrieved later by others.

Why is Sedona such a mysterious place, in the metaphysical sense?

Since it is a place where energy, knowledge and wisdom are stored, there must necessarily be access to them. In your now-time people can drive, take the plane, train, bus, horseback .... But how about in other times? How could they access places such as this? There are, as you know, time windows and, for that matter, spatial windows, that open up into this environment. It is, you might say, a massive portal to receive travelers from other dimensions, other times, other planets, other existences, and they are pouring through this area at all times. It is because of the energy here. You could create a portal where the energy is out of balance, but the moment you got into it you would be subject to the extremes of that energy. So, if you are coming from a very balanced world, perhaps a future or past time, you want to do the same thing all travelers do when they arrive at their destination: rest for a few moments and be able to adjust to the energies of the place. So you want your portal to exit into a place where there will be no immediate demands on you. This place and a few others around the world are that way even if there are visitors and people living here in your now dimension. Travelers must be able to come here to retrieve and to place information.

You may have had the experience of being inspired to do something that may not have had anything to do with the problem you were dwelling on. Very often a past or future life of yours — and you understand that they are of an infinite number — may come here because they see an advantage in your having an opportunity to receive inspiration from that lifetime. They cannot manipulate your life but they can create an opportunity for you to receive an inspiration, and then it is up to you as to whether to act on it or not. By acting on it you might benevolently affect your own life and, conceivably, past or future lives as well.

In the past several months there has been a tremendous amount of UFO activity here. Are they watching something?

An invitation has gone out to the galaxies and galaxies beyond them. It is a call to all those who can help balance the Earth and provide services to the populations of Earth who feel a greater connection to extraterrestial sources than to Earth herself. No less than 15 percent of all the people on the surface of the Earth right now would feel much more comfortable being on another planet than they feel here. And I do not mean that in a moment here or a moment there they would wish that. I mean that they always feel that way all the time. This means that the only way these people can be helped, can be inspired, is by extraterrestrial sources.

There is also a certain amount of assault going on. Government and science projects, through ultrasonic sound waves and high energy waves, although most often without intention, are creating discomfort for certain underground UFO bases that have been on this planet since before human beings were here. These people must be evacuated. Much of the talk of evacuation comes from this. These bases are being largely automated now and only individuals with tremendous immunity to these kinds of radiation are being left to maintain these bases. The lift-off of underground peoples has begun.

So many people who come to Sedona say they feel like they're coming home. Was there a civilization here, like Lemuria, to which people feel they are coming home?

Lemuria is a well-chosen term because the civilizations that most people of today identify with were here in the time of Mu, a civilization that slightly predated Lemuria. At that time the main tools of communication were sound, motion and a wave-form energy that travels easily under water. This area, at that time, was under water. A large ocean extended from what is now the Gulf up into Mexico and beyond into most of Arizona, part of New Mexico, a considerable portion of Southern California and a small portion of Nevada. This ocean also covered the Baja area of old Mexico. The water was saline but not as salty as the ocean is today. And the communication then was essentially a form of sound wave similar to that utilized by whales, dolphins and other sea creatures of today. Your scientists have observed this in the behavior of schools of fish who seem to turn on a dime without any apparent sound whatsoever. There's not enough sonic impulse to be measured since it is a form of magnetic sound energy. This kind of magnetic resonance is available here, especially because of the magnetism in the red rocks.

Yes, many people lived here in the culture of Mu which spread its cultural arm from what is now the Hawaiian Islands over to these shores — and there were shores in those days — and also through a series of underground rivers into several inland lakes, one of which is now called Lake Superior. Its field of influence stretched all the way over into what is now New Zealand, Australia, Japan, and through inland lakes and rivers, into North Korea and also parts of China and Mongolia.

So, you understand the ramifications. People who have had lives here and feel their resonance and the association to Lemuria, which is actually Mu, will also feel similar resonances where water streams travel. You might feel a similar resonance on the shores of Lake Superior or in Mongolia, for example.

Sedona is a region that stimulates the feeling of home in one's soul. Recognize that when you come here to visit, you are going to feel an attraction to seeking home. You might explore different regions and feel at home here but not there. Recognize that the intention is to create an identification in your body with the place of home.

Earth is your now home regardless of where you have traveled from the stars to become an Earth person. Mother Earth gives you your physical body from her own body. She wants you to feel at home here so you will have the same respect for your home, your planet, your body, that you would for your own physical home. Be welcome here; be at home here on Earth, as well as in Sedona, and feel the ordination you receive by being allowed to be physical, using the body of Mother Earth and the spirit of the Spirit that creates all life so that you might learn, grow, live, love and create a more beneficial and benevolent wisdom for your return.

Thank you.

Lyssa Royal / Germane

Lyssa is an internationally recognized channel whose work is seen regularly in such publications as *Connecting Link* and *Sedona Journal of Emergence!* She channels Germane, a group consciousness energy, whose orientation is from a realm of integration that does not have a clear-cut density/dimensional level.

Throughout time there have been many Sedonas on Earth, and even today there are several scattered around the planet. Sedona is a gateway to other dimensions and the energy in such a gateway profoundly affects the human body and consciousness. It's not just the etheric energy that forms the gateway which affects humans, but the unique combination of minerals (limestone, iron oxide, silicon dioxide) which form the magnificent rock formations, as well.

Individuals on your world who are in pursuit of spiritual development are often drawn to Sedona. When humans are receptive to the subtleties of energy and geophysical properties (as spiritual people often are), they seek out a physical environment which can stimulate their personal and spiritual growth even more profoundly. This attraction often exists on the subconscious level, and people seem to be mysteriously drawn. However, their souls and higher selves are leading them to the experiences of growth which can be stimulated by such powerful energies as those in Sedona.

Entities in other realms (both in physical forms and in nonphysical forms) are also attracted to the energy gateway of Sedona. When nonterrestrial entities wish to interact with Earth, they often use energetic "portholes" through which they can see into your reality. Sedona exists as a porthole through which other realms may observe and/or communicate. This explains some of the myriad of light phenomena, UFO sightings, and otherwise "strange" occurrences that Sedona is famous for. For there is a lot more going on around Sedona than is apparent to the eye!

There are many areas on your Earth which are considered sacred. Yet recognize that often the sacredness of a place can be entirely based on *human* creation. Sedona has been a sacred place since the time of Lemuria. It has held that sacredness through thousands of years of Native American tradition. After thousands of years of ceremony, spiritual recognition and pilgrimage, the very atmosphere around Sedona has become charged with a very strong energy that stimulates the human spirit. Sedona's sacredness will continue for millennia to come.

It has often been said about Sedona that miracles can happen there, or Sedona can chew you up and spit you out! This is because when one interacts with the energy in Sedona, all personal growth is magnified intensely. The more people deny or repress their pain (and thus what they wish to learn and heal), the more difficult a Sedona experience can be. Sedona is a mecca for all spiritual warriors! Our suggestion is that if you come to Sedona, suspend all expectation — for we guarantee that your stay will be filled with the unexpected!

Arthur Fanning / YHWH

Arthur Fanning, former Marine Corp captain and police officer, began his awakening in 1971, a process which continues to this day.
He channels YHWH
(Lord God Jehovah).

Why are so many spiritual people being drawn to the Sedona area and why is it such a mysterious place in a metaphysical sense?

Are you ready for this? It is beauteous country, and beings come forth earlier to be love nature, their movement here, understand. Then there became a love envelope understood here — nature. Now we are going to leap forward many years — eons or so — to your day now, to why it is becoming so popular. Lot of publicity. Now we will go back here.

Part of the wisdom of life manifested in this activity be ability to know gravity — how it works here, how you play it, how applied here. It is a process what you would term thought manipulation. That is all it is. In the ancient of times, to play in this activity, here, upon your planet, required a practice ground. And there be other places. Yet this be a place where the practice ground was sort of set so the stuckness would not be so grand upon. Other words, if you did your oops, you could still get out. Gravity — thought inverted, provided a what you call training field here for beings to participate, to understand how to play in reality third lowered, without playing the old game of doubt again. Doubt grand manipulator. So was built here system grid you term, not only above, within, of wire —you would call it lines, thicker, to play with, above and below. Avenues you call it — thought applied. In the ancient training ground, mankind, as he played, entities (I will say it in that manner) were free to leave at any moment if, what you call, they couldn't get it — desired not. They knew the road out. Does that answer your question?

Kind of, I guess. Why are so many people drawn here? There are people that are coming here that are just...

A lot of it be now out of fear that they have understood prior — this be way out. And your publicity.

Were there temples built here before Lemuria?

This place has been around a long time.

Will there be temples here in the future?

No more churches.

Good.

Thank you. Now in the understanding called temple, the word play here religion, indeed, yet there will be a form of the information available through here. Allowance for all. It'll be one of the transition points, so to speak, around — not what you call centered here, but it be path to move through for clearing. You're going to begin to find a lot of crystal moving upward out of the ground here. That is going to set off a rush.

Isn't there a crystal city in the records underground? Will we find that?

It is going to poke its way out. But there won't be that many beings here when it does.

Why are so many extraterrestrials and UFOs being drawn here?

They know of the line within. Now a lot of this thing, some want the best seat in the house, know you, when you watch ball game. They be around a lot of these places now. Now what you must understand — this be truly what be happening upon the planet is a spiritual understanding, awakening, that has not only significance for this what you call beauteous sphere; it is of galactic importance. And you are doing this thing. It is not that you are the bad guys last. Not at all. There are many beings here upon the planet we have taken upon meditations to what you call black holes and there be entities on the side of the hole — this side — that don't know what is on the other side. They are too afraid to go in. And they want to know when you come out what you saw. You are that powerful.

Love be the key, movement through, understanding. No name upon Source, All That Is, Father, God. Understanding Light that you are here. In that, you have the ability to move through all universes; not limited to stay. It is manipulation of body, be the tool out of the Light of your being. Not many qualified to participate. I know some of you think you were sent and stuck, but you all volunteered. Some of you even what you've called tricked someone to trick you into it so you would have someone to blame later. What you do, why, to be here now. The sooner you acknowledge that within your being, the more you will understand — the more of you. How? So get ready for a lot of fun with your electrical appliances here.

(Author's Note: Arthur Fanning was a medivac pilot in Vietnam. During a rescue mission, his helicopter was hit 360 times by machine-gun fire. The steering mechanism had been completely shot off — yet somehow, the helicopter landed safely. Obviously "someone" wanted Arthur around for a while.)

Index of Photographs

About
the Author

Tom Dongo

Tom Dongo is a long-time resident of Sedona. During this time, he has camped on and hiked over thousands of miles of the Sedona/Flagstaff/Prescott mountains, mesas, deserts, and canyons. He is a recognized world authority on UFOs and paranormal occurrences. He is also a writer of mainstream magazine articles and has written seven books on UFOs and the paranormal. His work and personal interviews have appeared many times on national and international television.

Light Technology PUBLISHING *Presents*

TO ORDER PRINT BOOKS

Visit LightTechnology.com, Call 928-526-1345 or 1-800-450-0985,
or Check Amazon.com or Your Favorite Bookstore

BOOKS BY TOM DONGO

Mysterious Sedona

It is well known among the curious that Sedona, Arizona, and its surrounding regions have seen some of the world's all-time, most intense UFO, paranormal, and spiritual activity. The question is, why?

This book explores deeply into that enigmatic activity.

"Tom Dongo has captured the essence of the UFO experience in Mysterious Sedona. As I read the firsthand reports of his repeated meeting with this bizarre phenomenon, I could actually feel his astonishment, fear, and wonderment. This marvelous book successfully combines the themes of horror and science fiction and would make a great novel, except for one fact: It is all true."

— Peter A. Gersten, attorney and director of Citizens Against UFO Secrecy

"Tom Dongo continues to amaze us with reports of strange airborne lights and vehicles, alien photos, mysterious men in underground tunnels, Bigfoot, and even a Sai Baba connection. I think Sedona has long been a place where old souls are guided, because there, a new paradigm is being born."

— Donald M. Ware, Truthseeker (and Colonel, U.S. Air Force, Retired)

Chapters Include

- Some Possible Explanations or — We May Not Be Who We Think We Are
- The Alien Tunnel System
- Back at the Ranch
- Another Strange Incident of the Two-Legged Kind
- The Incredible Sedona Lights
- Places to Look for the Sedona Lights
- Can It Get Any Stranger Than This?

$16.95 • Softcover • 144 PP.
978-1-62233-101-7

All Our Books Are Also Available as eBooks on Amazon, Apple, Google Play, Barnes & Noble, and Kobo.

Light Technology PUBLISHING *Presents*

TO ORDER PRINT BOOKS
Visit LightTechnology.com, Call 928-526-1345 or 1-800-450-0985,
or Check Amazon.com or Your Favorite Bookstore

BOOKS BY TOM DONGO

The Mysteries of Sedona

Learn about the esoteric side of Sedona that perhaps is being avoided by other writers, possibly for fear of ridicule, criticism, ostracism, and so on.

There are a lot of things going on in Sedona that are perhaps only being superficially touched on by much of the literature that is available. This book fills in that gap — and adds fuel to the fire.

To define Sedona in terms of principles of reality transcending those of any particular science, one could say that it is a town situated in a vast zone of powerful, shifting, mysterious, and sometimes volatile energies. To label these energies in only magnetic or electromagnetic terms is to restrict their greater meaning. These energies are truly cosmic and of many variations and applications. Energy emits in and around Sedona. Certain energies (vortexes) are at the moment in specific locations but can appear occasionally, or intensify, anywhere in the Sedona area. It is said that somehow Sedona's iron rich red rocks draw or generate these powers. It is said that these energies will soon expand and become one, then join with other energies and expand across the face of Earth.

THE
MYSTERIES
OF
SEDONA
THE NEW AGE FRONTIER
By Tom Dongo

Chapters Include
- Oak Creek Canyon
- The Metaphysical Community
- Sedona's Famous Vortexes
- Understanding, Experiencing, and Enjoying the Vortexes
- Channeling
- Sedona: the Re-emergence of Lemuria
- Spaceships and Paranormal Occurrences
- Sedona and the Days Ahead
- Indian Involvement
- Climate
- Rattlesnakes

$6.95 • Softcover • 96 PP.
978-0-9622748-0-0

All Our Books Are Also Available as eBooks on Amazon, Apple, Google Play, Barnes & Noble, and Kobo.

Light Technology PUBLISHING *Presents*

Dimensional Journey
by Linda Ball Bradshaw

Linda talks about her experiences amid Sedona's red rocks on Bradshaw Ranch and shares the spiritual guidance she received there. Linda came to realize that, like the high energy spots that exist on Earth, we also provide the setting for phenomena. We as human beings continually evolve, creating higher energy within ourselves. This works as a conduit for those who wish to observe another aspect of life within the cosmos.

This path we call life is filled with many wonderful experiences if we only realize how capable we really are of embarking on our very own dimensional journeys.

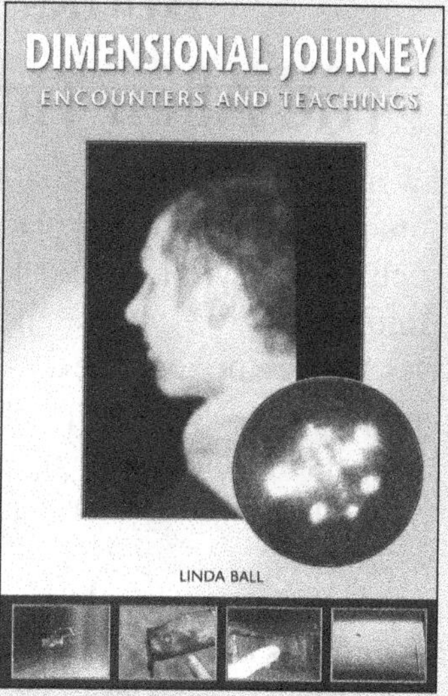

$19.95 • Softcover • 208 pp.
978-1-891824-34-0

THIRTY-TWO FULL-COLOR PAGES SHOWING OTHER-DIMENSIONAL & OFF-PLANET PHENOMENA

$4.95 • Softcover • 32 pp.
978-0-9622748-5-5

Everything You Wanted to Know About
Sedona in a Nutshell
by Tom Dongo

Oak Creek Canyon, Sedona Schnebly, geology, climate, metaphysical community, vortexes, UFOs, and real estate — this book covers it all.
Topics covered inside include:

- history
- Sedona Schnebly
- geology & climate
- Indian involvement
- arts & culture
- Sedona's famous vortexes
- UFOs over Sedona
- native trees & plants
- native wild animals
- rattlesnakes
- rock climbing & hiking
- camping
- backcountry tours
- clubs & churches
- restaurants
- motels
- golf
- sunrises & sunsets
- off-season
- jobs

✦ *Light Technology* PUBLISHING *Presents*

TO ORDER PRINT BOOKS
Visit LightTechnology.com, Call 928-526-1345 or 1-800-450-0985,
or Check Amazon.com or Your Favorite Bookstore

Echoes of Sedona Past

by Mary Lou Keller

A natural-born storyteller, Mary Lou Keller captured the wonder and magic of the Red Rock Country she loved as well as the living spirit of the Old West.

When Mary Lou organized the first metaphysical church in town, the Sedona Church of Light, she opened the doors to welcome many famous people of the day. In this book she brings to life the excitement of those early years of traveling gurus, spiritual teachers, psychic healers, and metaphysical happenings.

$14.95 • Softcover • 288 PP.
978-1-891824-22-7

SHIRT-POCKET SERIES

by Robert Shapiro

Feeling Sedona's ET Energies

Intended to support Earth and its people, this pocket-size book uses the energies in Sedona to motivate and stimulate potential actions.
$9.95 • Softcover • 96 PP.
978-1-891824-46-3

Touching Sedona

Speaks of Many Truths teaches how to communicate with the natural, powerful elements and wonders of Sedona in this pocket-size title.
$9.95 • Softcover • 96 PP.
978-1-891824-47-0

All Our Books Are Also Available as eBooks on Amazon, Apple, Google Play, Barnes & Noble, and Kobo.

Light Technology PUBLISHING *Presents*

TO ORDER PRINT BOOKS
Visit LightTechnology.com, Call 928-526-1345 or 1-800-450-0985,
or Check Amazon.com or Your Favorite Bookstore

BOOKS THROUGH DRUNVALO MELCHIZEDEK

THE ANCIENT SECRET OF THE FLOWER OF LIFE, VOLUME 1

Also available in Spanish as *Antiguo Secreto Flor de la Vida, Volumen 1*

Once, all life in the universe knew the Flower of Life as the creation pattern, the geometrical design leading us into and out of physical existence. Then from a very high state of consciousness, we fell into darkness, and the secret was hidden for thousands of years, encoded in the cells of all life.

$25.00 • 240 PP. • Softcover • ISBN 978-1-891824-17-3

THE ANCIENT SECRET OF THE FLOWER OF LIFE, VOLUME 2

Also available in Spanish as *Antiguo Secreto Flor de la Vida, Volumen 2*

Drunvalo shares the instructions for the Mer-Ka-Ba meditation, step-by-step techniques for the re-creation of the energy field of the evolved human, which is the key to ascension and the next dimensional world. If done from love, this ancient process of breathing prana opens up for us a world of tantalizing possibility in this dimension, from protective powers to the healing of oneself, others, and even the planet.

$25.00 • 272 PP. • Softcover • ISBN 978-1-891824-21-0

Includes Heart Meditation CD

LIVING IN THE HEART

Also available in Spanish as *Viviendo en el Corazón*

Long ago we humans used a form of communication and sensing that did not involve the brain in any way; rather, it came from a sacred place within our hearts. What good would it do to find this place again in a world where the greatest religion is science and the logic of the mind? Don't I know this world where emotions and feelings are second-class citizens? Yes, I do. But my teachers have asked me to remind you who you really are. You are more than a human being, much more. Within your heart is a place, a sacred place, where the world can literally be remade through conscious cocreation. If you give me permission, I will show you what has been shown to me.

— Drunvalo Melchizedek

$25.00 • 144 PP. • Softcover • ISBN 978-1-891824-43-2

🌱 *Light Technology* PUBLISHING *Presents*

TO ORDER PRINT BOOKS
Visit LightTechnology.com, Call 928-526-1345 or 1-800-450-0985,
or Check Amazon.com or Your Favorite Bookstore

PRODUCTS BY LYSSA ROYAL-HOLT

Galactic Heritage Cards

THE FIRST AND ONLY OF THEIR KIND: This 108-card divination system, based on material from Lyssa Royal-Holt's groundbreaking book *The Prism of Lyra*, is **designed to help you tap into your star lineage and karmic patterns** while revealing lessons brought to Earth from the stars and how those lessons can be used in your life on Earth now. Includes a 156-page book of instruction and additional information.

Illustrations by David Cow • 108 cards (2.75 x 4.5 inches)
156-page softcover book (4.5 x 5.5 inches) • $34.95 • 978-1-891824-88-3

Preparing for Contact
In this book, you will take an inner journey through your own psyche and discover a whole new dimension to your unexplained experiences.
$19.95 • Softcover • 320 PP.
978-1-891824-90-6

The Prism of Lyra
This text explores the idea that collective humanoid consciousness created this universe for specific purposes.
$16.95 • Softcover • 192 PP.
978-1-891824-87-6

The Golden Lake
This book features Pleiadian and Sirian awakening teachings that together provide a road map for the next phase of human evolution — the integration of polarity and the awakening of our consciousness beyond duality.
$19.95 • Softcover • 240 PP.
978-1-62233-070-6

All Our Books Are Also Available as eBooks on Amazon, Apple, Google Play, Barnes & Noble, and Kobo.

 Light Technology PUBLISHING *Presents*

SEDONA JOURNAL OF
Emergence

Find Answers to Satisfy Your Heart and Inspire Your Life in the #1 Channeled Magazine for Spiritual Guidance

In the *Sedona Journal of Emergence*, channeled lightbeings explain the process of your movement toward becoming your natural self and regaining your natural talents and abilities. They offer guidance to help you feel and express love and benevolence and to encourage you to make a difference in ensuring your expansion in consciousness as you move into another level of Earth — into the new reality.

The *Sedona Journal of Emergence* is the one monthly magazine you'll want to keep on hand!

- Mine the annual PREDICTIONS issue for insights on the coming year.
- Discover channeled information and inspired guidance intended to improve your body, mind, and soul.
- Learn how to improve yourself and, by default, help the planet.

DON'T DELAY — SUBSCRIBE TODAY!

SIGN UP ONLINE AT **SEDONAJOURNAL.COM**,
CALL 1-800-450-0985 OR 1-928-526-1345,

OR EMAIL **SUBSCRIPTIONS@LIGHTTECHNOLOGY.COM**.

(ELECTRONIC SUBSCRIPTIONS AVAILABLE)

Light Technology PUBLISHING Presents

EASY ORDER
24 HOURS A DAY

1 Order ONLINE!
LightTechnology.com

Order by Email
customersrv@lighttechnology.com

2 Order by Mail
Send to
Light Technology Publishing
PO Box 3540
Flagstaff, AZ 86003

3 Order by Phone
800-450-0985
928-526-1345

4 Order by Fax
928-714-1132

Available from your favorite bookstore or

LightTechnology.com
We Offer the Best Channeled and Inspired Books of Wisdom.
Use Our Secure Checkout.
In-Depth Information on Books, Including Excerpts and Contents.
Use the Links to Our Other Great Sites. See Below.

SedonaJournal.com
Read Excerpts of Monthly Channeling and Predictions in Advance.
Use Our Email Links to Contact Us or Send a Submission.
Electronic Subscriptions Available — with or without Print Copies.

BenevolentMagic.com
Learn the techniques of benevolence toward self and benevolence toward others to create global peace. Download all the techniques of benevolent magic and living prayer for FREE!

ExplorerRace.com
All humanity constitutes the Explorer Race, volunteers for a grand and glorious experiment. Discover your purpose, your history, and your future. Download the first chapter of each book for FREE!

ShamanicSecrets.com
What we call shamanism is the natural way of life for beings on other planets. Learn to be aware of your natural self and your natural talents and abilities. Download the first chapter of each book for FREE!